D1685663

The Great Northern Railway (Ireland) *in colour*

Norman Johnston

Dedicated to my Grandfather and Great-Grandfather, both of whom served the GNR with pride.

Norman Johnston has been a railway enthusiast for as long as he can remember, though with three earlier generations of Johnstons involved with transport, it was 'in the blood'. He began writing on railways in 1992 and has been the author, or joint author, of eight other railway books, including *The Fintona Horse Tram, Fermanagh's Railways, LNER Locomotives in colour, The Irish Narrow Gauge in colour* and, most notably, *Locomotives of the GNRI*.

Norman spent most of his working life in Co Tyrone before retiring from teaching in 1996 to concentrate on publishing and writing. He is a founder and joint partner of Colourpoint Books. He is married with two sons, both of whom are in the family publishing business.

Norman would especially like to thank a number of people who have assisted with this book, either by lending photographs and slides, assisting with drawings or reading the manuscript. In alphabetical order they are JG Dewing, Des FitzGerald, Charles Friel, Roger Joanes, Selwyn Johnston, John Langford, the late Keith Pirt, Arnold Richardson (Photobus), David Soggee, Joyce and Norman Topley, WFM Wallace, Ron White (Colour-Rail), Richard Whitford and Derek Young.

Designed by Colourpoint Books, Newtownards
Printed by W&G Baird Ltd

ISBN 1 904242 36 7

Colourpoint Books
Jubilee Business Park
21 Jubilee Road
NEWTOWNARDS
County Down
Northern Ireland
BT23 4YH
Tel: 028 9182 0505
Fax: 028 9182 1900
E-mail: info@colourpoint.co.uk
Web-site: www.colourpoint.co.uk

Front cover: VS 4-4-0 No 209 *Foyle* approaches Killester with a Sunday morning express for Belfast on 27 September 1958. The GNR is within days of being dissolved and already the engine and stock have been stenciled 'CIE'.
JG Dewing/Colour-Rail IR317

Back cover:

Top: In September 1957 PPs 4-4-0 No 12 arrives at Fintona Junction with a train from Omagh to Enniskillen. The line to the right continued down to Fintona and no doubt the photographer had just arrived from the town in the famous horse tram.
Ray Oakley/Colour-Rail IR601

Bottom: A detail of the nameplate and splasher of S class 4-4-0 No 174 *Carrantuohill*. Note the 1939 works plate dating from the renewal of the engine.
John Langford

Title page: The south end of Strabane in GNR days. In slightly dusty blue livery is S2 class 4-4-0 No 192 *Slievenamon*. The GNR favoured centre corridor Third class accomodation and two such vehicles head the rake, followed by a steel-sided Composite and Buffet Car. Bringing up the rear are a Mail Van and a strengthening Open Third.
Ray Oakley/Colour-Rail

CONTENTS

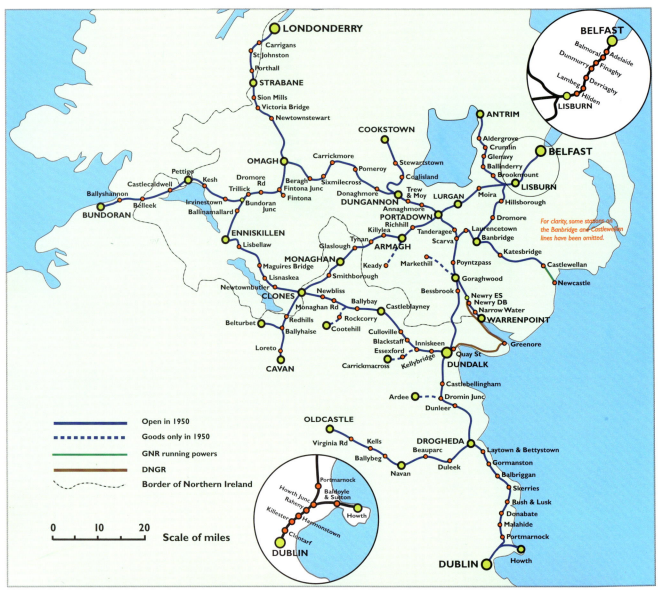

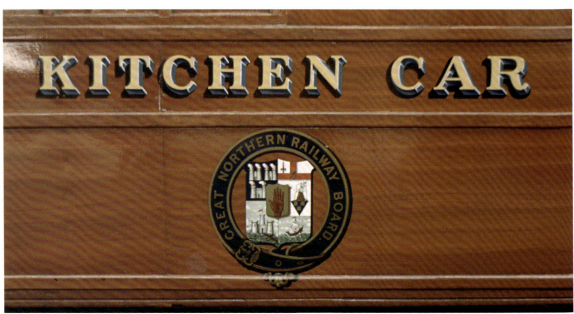

A GNRB crest on the side of Kitchen Car No 399 at Great Victoria Street on 6 May 1959. This shows the panelling and the painted and scumbled mahogany effect to good advantage. The 'Board' crest was in use from 1953 to 1958. Prior to that, crests carried '(Ireland)' instead of 'Board'.

JG Dewing

4

INTRODUCTION

It is probably the case that the last thing to be read in most transport books is the Introduction – unless it is very short! I am also sure that, for the majority of my readers, the GNR(I) needs no introduction. I do not intend, therefore, to give any kind of potted history of the company.

Anyone who has read my earlier *Locomotives of the GNRI* (Colourpoint 1999) or my joint book with Charles Friel, *Fermanagh's Railways* (Colourpoint 1998), will know that I am a passionate enthusiast for all things Great Northern. This seems to have been so from a very early age.

Up to 1953, all of my early train trips had been on the Great Northern and I had assumed that the GNRI was the company which ran *all* the railways in Northern Ireland. That summer my father, who worked for the road transport part of the Ulster Transport Authority in Portadown, announced that we were going to Portrush for our holiday, and that most of the journey would be by *UTA* train. I remember being incredulous that the UTA had *trains*. To me the UTA meant buses and lorries and to convince me he showed me a map in the UTA timetable, where lines to Portrush, Larne and Bangor were green. This was education at its most painful! However, I want to make it very clear to my NCC friends that the trip to Portrush was most impressive and I bear no malice against the NCC. It was just . . . er, different.

The purpose of this particular book is to present an all-colour portrait of the GNR, as it was in the 1950s. In Colourpoint, our first foray into all colour albums in this format was *Isle of Man Classic Steam* (1998), followed by the two albums on *The Wee Donegal* (1998 and 2002) and then *The Irish Narrow Gauge* (2003). We felt it was now time to turn to the 'five foot three' and we hope to follow up this album in coming years with a similar book on the UTA.

Creating a colour album devoted exclusively to the GNR(I) is something of a challenge, as material is necessarily scarce. I remember when the first commercially available colour slides came on the market in the late 1960s, mainly from Colourviews and CCQ. At that time you were pleased to get pictures of U class 4-4-0s in UTA black with green coaches. Actual GNR-era slides were a dream and, when the first two slides of blue U class engines at Bundoran shed and on the 'Bundoran Express' were offered, Heaven had arrived! One is reproduced in this book, on page 111.

An interesting comparison between two views of No 174 *Carrantuohill*.

As built in 1913 (above) the engine was in green livery and had Ramsbottom safety valves, soon replaced by the Ross Pop type. Note the bogie splasher, the pipe for the exhaust steam injector, the sander to the rear drivers and the frames painted red/brown. The device on the smokebox is a superheater damper piston with its control rod running to the cab.

The June 1961 view at Cork (right) shows the same engine as renewed in 1939. Apart from the livery, many differences are noticeable. The renewal resulted in a virtually new engine with new frames (of a different shape), new boiler and long travel valves, producing a very free-running engine.

Railway Magazine, Sept 1913 (above)/
John Langford (right)

Things have moved on a lot since those days and in this album you will see slides of five different Qs class engines. Slides of relatively obscure classes, such as QLs, PGs, AL and QGT2, are now regarded as normal. The good news is that there were about a hundred slides available which I have not included, leaving aside ones that were ruled out because they have already been published in other books. Should this album lead to previously unknown photographers offering their material for publishing, perhaps there might some day be a *GNR(I) Revisited*.

I set myself broad parameters for this album. I have tried to offer new material, though I have made some exceptions where I felt they were justified. The slides had to have an authentic 'GNR feel' to them so, as well as pre-October 1958 views, material from 1959–62 was accepted, provided the engine, and most of the carriages, were in GNR livery, even if the dreaded stencils 'UT' or 'CIE' appeared on the buffer beams. In a few cases the UTA has renumbered the engines or carriages but, by and large, the visual impact is still GNR. Only one GNR engine in UTA black crept in and there are no ex-NCC engines. There are two main exceptions to the 'no CIÉ or UTA' rule. One was that material on the Irish North and the Oldcastle line was so scarce that I had to accept trains which, although of GNR stock, were in CIÉ green. The second broad exception was for station exteriors, views of stations with no trains and 'out of the window' shots where the only views available show the stations in the early 1960s. Thus some station views as late as 1963–64 appear but, apart from paint, the infrastructure is still largely as it was in the GNR era.

Inevitably, I was restricted by what the featured photographers preferred to photograph or were on time to record. Thus, blue engines feature strongly, even though only 28 engines out of about 190 were blue. Locomotive portraits were often the most popular type of photograph, but today are regarded as amongst the least interesting. I have largely confined these to the locomotive survey.

In retrospect, general views and slides featuring carriages as well as engines are the most absorbing. The vast majority of shots featured Belfast, Portadown, Dundalk, Drogheda, Dublin and, rather oddly, Strabane. Thus, pictures at smaller stations – even some not so small – are like hen's teeth. Did no one ever photograph Lisburn or Lurgan before 1959, for instance? Oddly, although photographers seem to have visited the Irish North regularly, and always covered the Fintona tram, I have only ever seen one colour photo of the Portadown–Clones line, which closed on the same day. Apart from one shot of the lifting train, my coverage of this route has been confined to some excellent 1961–62 views of the closed stations. Conversely, I have been able to provide 18 views of the hitherto virtually uncovered Oldcastle branch and a few new shots of the Belturbet branch. Sadly, I was unable to find anything on the lines to Banbridge, Newcastle and Cookstown which closed in 1955–56.

Always mindful of the needs of modellers, I have included track diagrams of major stations, though I must stress that, apart from Dundalk, these are not to scale. There is also a carriage section and plenty of views showing the colour of brick and stone work, station signage, etc.

Anyway, as they say in Northern Ireland, "Nuf said." It is time for me to call a halt to this ramble and let you get on with poring over the pictures. Enjoy your read!

A superb study of Qs class 4-4-0 No 131 heading the 8.10am Belfast–Dublin away from Drogheda on Friday 15 May 1959. The second carriage is a B¹ Dining Car, built in 1925.

The bridge beyond the train spanned both the main line and Buckey's sidings, to the right behind the trees.

Other items of interest are the vertical white board on the signal post to aid sighting and the white hexagon indicating the presence of track circuiting.

JG Dewing

STEAM LOCOMOTIVES

This section is intended to be a brief introduction to the different types of GNR locomotive that will feature in this book. My comments will describe the situation that pertained from the mid 1950s. Most GNR locomotives were inside cylindered 4-4-0s of varying vintage for passenger work and similar 0-6-0s for goods work. The commonest tank engines were 4-4-2Ts, with a smattering of other types.

The oldest engines still running in the 1950s were the A class 0-6-0s. Introduced by James Park in 1882, 15 were built up to 1891 but only Nos 28, 33, 60 and 150 survived to the 1950s. Here, the very last, No 150, awaits cutting up at Dundalk in June 1961, looking like an engine with five tenders. To the right is a former railmotor coach, then in use with the locomotive department.
RA Biddick/Colour-Rail

The A class were followed by the slightly larger AL class in 1893–96. Eleven were built and all survived until 1957. The letter 'A' on the cab denotes the power classification, not the engine class. The A and AL classes both had 17"x 24" cylinders but the AL class had a longer wheelbase. No 58 is shunting at Dundalk in July 1956. It was built in 1896 and withdrawn by CIÉ in October 1959.
Keith Pirt

The oldest 4-4-0s in the 1950s were James Park's P6'6" class, of which there were four – Nos 26, 27 (1892) and 72, 73 (1895). Superheated in the 1930s, they were mainly seen on the Irish North section. No 27 poses impressively in Dundalk shed yard in July 1956. No 26 was withdrawn in 1957 and the other three by CIÉ in 1959. It is unlikely that any of them ran after the closure of the Irish North in October 1957. The white diamond on the buffer beam denoted a maximum loco axle weight of 15.2 tons. *Keith Pirt*

Contemporary with the P6'6" class were the eight smaller-wheeled P5'6" 4-4-0s. Nos 51–54 (1892–95) were withdrawn in 1950 and Nos 88, 89 (1904) and 104 (1906) in 1956, leaving only No 105 (also 1906). The class was at one time associated with the Banbridge and Newcastle line, but in its last years No 105 was used in such far-flung places as Cavan and Omagh. Here it is at Portadown in May 1956, probably on a Armagh train. The veteran carriage set has been strengthened by a K[15] Open Third AEC railcar trailer. No 105 passed to CIÉ and was withdrawn in 1960. *AD Hutchinson/Colour-Rail IR565*

The oldest tank engines in the 1950s were the six JT class 2-4-2Ts, Nos 90–95. They too were a Park design and were built in 1895–1902. Originally suburban tanks, they were relegated to branch line duties in their later lives. The closure of the Dundalk, Newry and Greenore Railway on the last day of 1951 made most of them redundant and all were withdrawn in 1955–57, except for No 91 which was retained for the Belturbet branch. Built at Dundalk in 1902, it is seen in excellent condition at Belturbet in July 1956 and continued in use as a shunter with CIÉ until about 1961. Although No 91 was scrapped in 1963, No 93 of the class is preserved at the Ulster Folk and Transport Museum, Cultra, Co Down.   *Keith Pirt*

In 1895 Park retired as Locomotive Superintendent and was replaced by Charles Clifford who held the post until 1912. In 1896 he introduced the popular PP class which was developed from the P6'6" class and built until 1911. Seventeen were built, though with many variations at first. By 1945, rebuilding had turned them into a homogeneous class with 6'7" driving wheels, 18"x 24" cylinders and (apart from 129) a beefy 4'6" superheated boiler. All survived until 1957 and they were universal on the Irish North lines and branch line services elsewhere. No 42 is resting between duties at Strabane on 7 March 1958. Most were gone by 1960 but No 74 lasted with the UTA until 1963.

WP de Beer/Colour-Rail

Contemporary with the PP class were the seven PG class 0-6-0s, which were in power group 'B'. They were Nos 10, 11, 100–103 and 151. Four were built at Dundalk in 1899–1904 and Nos 101–103 by Neilson Reid at Glasgow in 1901. One of the latter is seen at Newry, Edward Street, on 16 March 1959. All passed to the UTA and were withdrawn in 1960–61, except No 10 which lasted until 1964.

Alan Chandler/Colour-Rail

In 1899 the much larger Q class 4-4-0 was introduced and was the first of what I call the 'Q family'. These were Nos 120–25 (1902–04 in reverse order) and 130–36 (1899–1900, likewise). No 125 is seen at Adelaide shed, Belfast on 8 June 1957, fitted with a staff net for use on the Derry Road, where these rugged engines were popular. As rebuilt, they had 6'7" driving wheels, 18½"x 26" cylinders, superheaters and piston valves. Withdrawal was between 1957 and 1963, the last survivors being Nos 131, 132 and 135. No 131 is preserved at Whitehead and may eventually be restored.

K Cooper/Colour-Rail

The goods version of the Q class were the QG 0-6-0s, of which only four were built, Nos 152–55 in 1903–04. Their low pitched boilers give some idea of the proportions of the Q class before rebuilding in 1919–24. When superheated, the QGs retained slide valves and were in power group 'B'. The GNR was unusual compared to some English railways in superheating most of their 0-6-0s and even some shunting engines. All QGs passed to CIÉ and were withdrawn in 1962, except No 152, which lasted a year longer and is seen shunting the Brewery sidings at Dundalk on 19 May 1962.

JG Dewing/ Colour-Rail IR314

The GNR relied largely on tender engines for shunting, but built some shunting tanks for use in Dublin and Belfast. Nos 98 and 99 (Robert Stephenson 1905) were a 0-6-2 tank version of the QG 0-6-0 and thus QGT. They were superheated in the 1930s. No 98 was withdrawn in 1957 but No 99 survived until 1960, having passed to CIÉ in 1958. In this view it is marshalling a cattle train at Sheriff Street goods yard, Dublin on 4 May 1957. A six wheel Belgian-built brake van forms part of the consist. The GNR's Amiens Street signal cabin dominates the background.

ES Russell/Colour-Ra

Another pair of 0-6-2Ts, Nos 168 and 169, were built in 1911. These were to a modified design, the QGT2 class, and had larger fireboxes. They were built to shunt a new modern goods marshalling yard at Adelaide, Belfast. Designed as two sets of converging loops, the yard required a powerful tank engine at the Lisburn end of the arrivals side and at the Belfast end of the departures side. Neither were ever superheated and were withdrawn in 1957, after many years in storage. No 169 had been out of use since 1953 when photographed at Dundalk in July 1956. *Keith Pirt*

QLs 4-4-0 No 156 leaves Belfast with a Newry train about 1957. There were originally eight of the QL type, built in 1904–10 with larger boilers than the Qs. Although fitted with piston valves and superheaters in their final form, their boilers were pitched lower than the Qs as the valves were between the cylinders, rather than above. Their large fireboxes made them heavy on coal despite their modest duties. No 114 was scrapped in 1932, and Nos 24, 113, 126 and 128 in 1957, leaving only Nos 126, 156 and 157 to pass to the UTA. These went in 1959–60. Note Dining Car No 403 in AEC railcar livery; it later became UTA/NIR No 554. *Colour-Rail*

The goods version of the QLs were the impressive LQGs, which were power group 'D' and, in tractive effort terms, the most powerful engines on the GNR (25,270 lbs). They had 4'7¼" driving wheels and 19"x 26" cylinders. Popularly known as 'rebuilt Ds', there were originally 11 in the class when built in 1906–08. However, in later years, four members of the 1911 NQG and LNQG classes were later absorbed into the LQG class, bringing the total to 15. This useful class was still intact in 1958 and the last was scrapped in 1964. On 10 May 1962, CIÉ-owned No 164 steams past Drogheda South cabin. Note the cement dust on the tyres. *B Oatway*

RT class 0-6-4T No 166 is seen at Adelaide shed on Saturday 8 June 1957. The 'R family' was a rather small one – one class with four members. Nos 22 and 23 were built in 1908 and Nos 166 and 167 in 1911. In a sense, these engines were a tank version of the AL 0-6-0s and were designed for dock shunting, with small 4'3" wheels and cut down boiler mountings. They spent their working lives in the Belfast docks. Oddly, despite their rear bogies, they were smaller than the 0-6-2Ts. All passed to the UTA, with No 22 going in 1959 and the others in 1963.

K Cooper/Colour-Rail

In 1912 Charles Clifford retired and was succeeded as Locomotive Superintendent by George Glover, an NER Gateshead man. The S class had been designed by Clifford but changes were made by Glover before completion in 1913. These were the first superheated express engines on the GNR but they were completely renewed in 1938–39. Five were built, Nos 170–74, with 6'7" wheels and 19"x 26" cylinders. After renewal they had the attractive sky blue livery and were named after Irish mountains. No 174 looks reasonably clean at Adelaide on 8 June 1957. The RPSI-owned No 171 is, of course, the best known member of the class.

K Cooper/Colour-Rail

The SG class was the 0-6-0 version of the S class 4-4-0, but with a sloping grate in contrast to the horizontal type on the S class. Nos 175–79 were built in 1913. A very clean No 177 is running round a train at Oldcastle on 28 April 1962.

The SG class and all subsequent 0-6-0s had 5'1" wheels, compared to the 4'7" of earlier types. These engines were power class 'C' and were superheated from new.

Richard Whitford

In 1915 the three-strong Class S2 was built. Nos 190–92 were very similar to the S class, but had inclined valves and direct link motion, as opposed to the horizontal valves and rocker arms of the S and SG classes. In 1938–39, they were renewed, receiving blue livery and mountain names. This interesting view shows No 190 *Lugnaquilla* at Strabane on 15 May 1958, shunting a cattle truck on or off the rear of a BUT railcar bound for Derry. The unique tender on No 190, with its higher coal capacity, dated from trials for the non-stop 'Enterprise' in 1947. Note the busy narrow gauge Co Donegal platform on the left and the couple on the right using the barrow path to avoid the footbridge.
Chris Gammell/Colour-Rail

The cab of No 190, pictured on 2 August 1958, illustrates the typical layout of GNR footplates, normally arranged for left hand drive. Note the prominent Beyer Peacock builder's name behind the regulator. one of many components recycled during Dundalk Works 'renewal' of the S and S2 class locomotives.
ES Russell/Colour-Rail

The goods equivalent of the S2 class was the ten strong SG2 class, with the same valve arrangement as the passenger engines. Nos 180–84 were built by Beyer Peacock in 1915 and Nos 15–19 by Nasmyth Wilson in 1924. One of the latter is illustrated here with its distinctive triangular works plate on the leading splasher. No 18 is having a rest at Drogheda shed in July 1956, possibly on a Sunday afternoon, with an NQG facing it. The SG and SG2 classes were withdrawn in 1961–65, apart from No 19, scrapped in 1959.
Keith Pirt

The ultimate development of the S family were the 'Big Ds', or SG3 class. These had 19½"x 26" cylinders and 5'0" boilers and were the favoured type for heavy Derry Road goods trains. Fifteen were built by Beyer Peacock in 1920–21, using scattered numbers between 6 and 202. Here No 8 shows its impressive lines at Grosvenor Road goods yard, Belfast, in July 1956. The first withdrawals were in 1961, with most UTA examples lasting until 1965. No 97 was not cut up until 1970. *Keith Pirt*

Going back to 1913, we now trace the development of the T and U families. Glover saw the need for lighter engines for suburban and branch line work and introduced the T class (later T1) 4-4-2Ts in 1913. Nos 185–89 had 18"x 24" cylinders, 5'9" driving wheels and bogie brakes. As built, they were unsuperheated. They spent most of their lives on suburban passenger duties in the Dublin and Belfast areas. Here No 186 and her fireman pose at Amiens Street shed in July 1956. All but one were withdrawn in 1959–60, No 187 surviving as a shunter at Belfast until 1964.

K Cooper/Colour-Rail IR383

The success of the T1 class led to the introduction of a tender version in 1915, the light U class 4-4-0 which, with its lower axle loading, was more suitable for the branch lines. Nos 196–200 were built by Beyer Peacock in 1915 and were popularly known as the 'Irish North engines'. They had 5'9" driving wheels and 18"x 24" cylinders.

Originally black and unnamed, after 1948 they received the blue livery and were named after loughs. A fairly presentable No 199 *Lough Derg* is out of steam at Amiens Street shed on Saturday 16 May 1959. It was withdrawn by CIÉ in November 1962.

JG Dewing

The T1 class was followed by the superheated T2 class in 1921–30. Other than by their numbers it is very hard to distinguish the two classes. The main external differences were in the cab and bunker, the entrance to the T2 footplate being nearer the bunker. This was the most numerous class of GNR engine. Five (Nos 1–5) were built by Beyer Peacock in 1921, ten (scattered numbers) by Nasmyth Wilson in 1924 and five (Nos 62–66) by Beyer Peacock in 1930. They were very common in the Belfast and Dublin areas, operating to Howth, Drogheda, Lisburn, Portadown, Armagh and Newry. However, they were rarely seen on the Derry line or Irish North branches. Fifteen were withdrawn in 1959–60, having been displaced by the diesels and two more in 1961. The last of them were Nos 3, 5 and 143. No 30, seen here at Adelaide in May 1957, was withdrawn in December 1961. *JG Dewing/Colour-Rail IR307*

The goods version of the U class, the UG 0-6-0, did not appear until 1937, They were not given power classification letters, but would have been 'B'. George B Howden had replaced Glover in 1933 but his background was civil engineering and locomotive matters were mainly handled by his assistant, HR McIntosh, who himself became Locomotive Engineer in 1939. McIntosh introduced a new style of cab, with a square window (initially glazed) in place of a cut out. These light 0-6-0s were excellent mixed traffic engines and did much suburban passenger work under the UTA. Nos 78–82 were built in 1937 and Nos 145–49, to a slightly modified design, in 1948. They were rarely photographed in colour in GNR days and perhaps the state of No 81 in this 1956 view at Adelaide suggests why. *Keith Pirt*

In 1947, McIntosh ordered a further five U class from Beyer Peacock. These picked up some of the design cues of the 1937 UGs, including the square cab cut out. They also had modern LMS-style 2500 gallon roller-bearing tenders. Named after counties in which the GNR operated, and delivered in January 1948, Nos 201–05 were the last inside-cylindered 4-4-0s to be built in the world. No 202 *Louth* is shunting near Dundalk Central Cabin about 1958. It was withdrawn by the UTA in 1965. *Reg Ludgate/Colour-Rail*

Odd man out in the GNR fleet was No 31, the 0-6-0 crane tank, built in 1928. Seen here in steam at Dundalk in 1956, attached to a runner wagon (to protect other rolling stock) and with a tantalising glimpse of the MAK diesel in the background, it was a typical Hawthorn Leslie industrial tank. For a time it was the only GNR engine with outside cylinders and was the Dundalk Works shunter and mobile crane. The coal bunker was added in May 1950. In 1958 the works became a private engineering firm and sold No 31 to CIÉ in 1960. It was scrapped in 1965 without seeing any further use.

Keith Pirt

The first really modern express engines built for the GNR were Nos 83–87, the V class three cylinder compounds, built in 1932. They were compounded on the Smith system, as used on the NER and LMS 4-4-0s. Named after birds of prey, and at first black, they were the first to get the blue livery from May 1936. Inevitably this led to the nickname 'Bluebirds' with obvious Malcolm Campbell inspiration. This view shows No 83 *Eagle* ex-works at Dundalk on 31 July 1953, though coupled to a far-from-fresh tender. Originally built with round-topped boilers (see page 44), they all received Belpaire fireboxes in 1946–50. Readers will be familiar with the now-preserved RPSI No 85 *Merlin*, the only active mainline compound in these islands.

K Cooper/Colour-Rail

The heavy post-war traffic led McIntosh to order five more three-cylinder engines, which came from Beyer Peacock in 1948 and were the last new 4-4-0s in the world. However, Nos 206–10 were built as simples and in most respects were very up to date – Walshaerts valve gear, 4000 gallon roller bearing tenders and, soon after introduction, smoke deflectors. Oddly McIntosh reverted to a cab with a cutout and uniquely for the GNR they had number plates. No 207 *Boyne* is seen at Amiens Street shed in June 1961, running without lettering as it had been overhauled at Dundalk in 1959 under CIÉ ownership. This engine missed preservation by a whisker. It was rumoured in 1965 that Sir Billy Butlin wanted to display it at Mosney Holiday Camp.

Keith Pirt

DIESEL TRAINS

The contribution of the GNR to the development of diesel traction has already been well-documented in Colm Flanagan's excellent *Diesel Dawn* (Colourpoint 2003) and my own *Locomotives of the GNRI* (1999). My purpose here is to illustrate the main types of GNR diesel train, most of which appear again elsewhere in the book. The only type which did not last into the 1950s was Railcar B, which ran as a carriage from 1946. Withdrawn in 1949, it lay at Dundalk for many years.

Railcar A was, of course, the pioneer and remained a useful unit right into the 1960s, mainly because it had two cabs. Built in 1932, it was long associated with the Scarva–Banbridge branch, but was transferred to the Oldcastle branch when the former line closed in 1955. This explains why our picture shows it at Drogheda shed yard in July 1956. In later years it saw service on local trains on the Derry Road, and was even re-engined in 1961. After damage in a shunting accident in 1963, it was sold to a contractor and used on lifting trains up to at least 1969.

Keith Pirt

There were three articulated railcars with single cabs – C[1] (1934), C[2] and C[3] (both 1935) – but all slightly different. In the 1950s they operated local trains on the Irish North, the Bundoran branch, the Derry Road and the Oldcastle branch. Light in construction, eccentric in appearance and limited by needing turned each journey, they saw little use after the closure of the Irish North in 1957. Here Railcar C[2] lies at Dundalk on 9 June 1961, alongside sister C[1].

Colour-Rail

There were four articulated railcars in the more versatile layout of a central engine unit, with a carriage body and cab articulated at each end. These, and all the cars illustrated earlier, had Gardner engines. D and E were built in 1936 and by the 1950s were usually on the Warrenpoint branch. Their power bogies were six-coupled. In 1938 cars F and G appeared. They had two-axle power bogies with direct drive from two smaller engines and were used mainly on the suburban service from Dublin to Howth. However, in 1958, F passed to the UTA and, on 17 May 1960, it is passing under what would eventually be the M1 bridge between Finaghy and Dunmurry on the 12.30pm service to Newry Edward Street.

JG Dewing

The GNR also converted a number of road buses to rail use. Four of these quaint vehicles (Nos 1–3 and 8177) were still in use in the 1950s, mainly on the Irish North and the branch to Oldcastle. No 8177 (previously No 4) was in departmental service and is seen here on Dundalk shed turntable in 1956. It was converted to rail use in 1935 as DNGR No 2, entered GNR stock in 1948 and was scrapped in 1961. No 3, scrapped in 1955 had been DNGR No 1. Note the steel wheel at the front of No 8177, but rubber tyre inside a steel rim on the rear axle. No 1 (see page 81) later entered departmental stock as No 8178, probably about 1958, and is now preserved at the Ulster Folk and Transport Museum, Cultra.

Keith Pirt

In 1950 the GNR introduced a fleet of 20 Park Royal diesel railcars with underfloor AEC engines. The policy of identifiing railcars as E, F, G, etc, was thankfully abandoned as there were only 19 letters left! The new cars were numbered 600–19 and were the first fleet of multiple unit railcars in these islands, other than four GWR examples. This very early view, on 26 June 1952, shows No 605 and an L[13] trailer at the rear of Adelaide shed, where they were initially serviced. This shows the original livery scheme with the side fleet number above the front bogie.

I Davidson/Colour-Rail

The later livery is illustrated by this view of No 600 after repainting, probably about 1955. Note that the side number is now carried towards the rear. Buffers, engines and bogies were traditionally painted silver. One popular feature of these cars was that first class gave a panoramic view forward over the driver's shoulder. This was less popular with drivers! The AEC cars were wired for only two-car control. The UTA later modified them to full DMU status with up to four power cars.

JG Wallace/Colour-Rail

A rear view of ex-works car No 603 about 1958, verified by the stenciled 'UT' on the end. The guard's compartment had a boiler for steam-heating and some space for luggage, but railcar sets often hauled a four-wheel van for the extensive parcels and mail traffic. Note the BUT railcar in the left background and not a steam train in sight at Great Victoria Street in 1958! The blue and cream livery was carried round coach ends, unlike the normal mahogany finish. No 603 became UTA and NIR No 111 and was withdrawn in 1973.

Reg Ludgate/Colour-Rail

The final design of GNR railcar appeared in 1957 and this was one of the first trains that I ever saw running on its first day in service. Twenty four cars were equipped by BUT (the successor to AEC), and completed at Dundalk, in 1957–58. Nos 701–16 had a small cab at each end, allowing through corridor connections and were completed first. An unidentified car of this type is seen at Strabane, heading towards Portadown, on 2 August 1958. These cars had unusual continental-style rubber corridor connections which were not compatible with AEC-fitted or hauled stock.

ES Russell/Colour-Rail

The last eight cars were numbered 901–08 and had a cab at one end only. As this was full-width, these cars were intended to be the leading, or end, vehicles of diesel trains. On the Derry Road, BUT trains usually ran as six-car sets with three or four power cars. Here No 907 (running as UTA No 135) is at the head of a Belfast train at Strabane in mid-1959, with a similar car at the rear. 700-series cars are second and fourth in the formation. The headlight on BUT cars was positioned higher than on the AECs.

Keith Bannister/Colour-Rail

CARRIAGES

In the 1950s the GNR had an enormously interesting collection of carriages. Virtually every bogie carriage built since 1889 was still running in 1951, except for those lost to accidents or fire. Few new carriages, other than diesel railcars and trailers, were built in the 1950s, but the growing summer excursion traffic after the war frustrated efforts by the GNR to dispose of obselete vehicles and modernise the fleet.

The last GNR six-wheelers, other than brake vans, were withdrawn in 1948 but one interesting survivor into the 1950s was No 8453, the Locomotive Department engineman's instruction coach, seen in the scrap line at Inchicore in March 1962. Rebuilt from a standard six-wheeled Third in 1920, the coach probably dated from the early 1880s. It was used to house working models of engine valve gear, cylinders, lubricators, boilers and other equipment relevant to enginemen, including a model railway with signals. *David Soggee*

The GNR officially recognised four carriage roof profiles, which were 'flat' (really shallow arc and used mainly on six-wheelers), 'low elliptical', 'clerestory' and 'high elliptical'. Examples of the last three were common in the 1950s and M² class bogie brake No 240, seen at Great Victoria Street sidings, Belfast, in 1958, is an example of 'low elliptical'. Stock of this type was built in the period 1893–1902. No 240 was built in 1901 and withdrawn in 1960. Two of this class of four were converted to B⁷ kitchen cars in 1940.

Reg Ludgate/Colour-Rail

This interesting rake of stored carriages at Sutton in March 1959 includes examples of clerestory and low elliptical-roofed vehicles in the foreground. Over the winter months the GNR stored large numbers of older vehicles like this at various locations around the system. These were pressed into service in the summer for seaside excursions or Orangemen's specials during the Northern Ireland 'marching season'. In the case of the vehicles seen here, the scrap line will be their next destination. The second vehicle is a K[1] Third, which seated 100 in ten compartments with limited leg room, in a vehicle only 51'3" long. *John Langford*

Compartment stock was still widely used for suburban trains in the late 1950s, as seen here at Amiens Street, Dublin on 14 June 1959. The engine is SG3 0-6-0 No 48, with a 1948 UG tender. Clerestory-roofed stock was built in 1895–1910. No 49 is an F[13] Composite from 1905 – note the wider First Class compartments. Next is K[3] Third No 126 of 1908, which at one time had two central toilets, accessible only from the adjacent compartments. Nearest the engine is I[13] No 270, a rather rare Tricomposite Corridor, built in 1929. *AG Cramp/Colour-Rail*

Some more modern high elliptical compartment stock was built in the 1920s, mainly for first and second class season ticket holders. A good example is F[2] Composite No 354 of 1921, which is running as an all-first and in this view has been renumbered N281 by the UTA, though still retaining its GNR crest. Originally only the two centre compartments were first class. GNR Composites were 1st/2nd rather than 1st/3rd, as second class was retained until 1 January 1951. *Derek Young*

Dining cars operated on Belfast–Dublin and Belfast–Londonderry services, along with buffet or teacars and catering vehicles could also be found on the 'Bundoran Express' and some special workings like rugby specials and mystery trains. Most GNR Dining Cars were end-kitchen layout but B[5] No 144, with its centre kitchen, was an exception. Built in 1916 as an Inspection Saloon, it became a Dining Car in 1927. Here it is coupled to a B[7] Kitchen Car.

WE Robertson/Colour-Rail

The GNR was unusual among mainline railways in these islands in prefering the centre corridor layout rather than the more normal side corridor. Side corridor was used for superior accomodation after 1916, but centre corridor remained the norm for Thirds. No third class side corridor vehicles were built until 1932 and only five after that date. Class K[11] Third No 441 was photographed at Strabane in August 1958 and is a good example of the centre-corridor type. The compartments seated 16 and were joined by interconnecting doors. This view also illustrates well the GNR mahogany-effect paint finish, which used the 'scrumble' method to imitate wood grain.

ES Russell/Colour-Rail

This June 1959 view at Dublin shows one of the attractive K[13] side-corridor panelled Thirds built in 1932 for the mainline expresses. This example has just been renumbered N382 by the UTA but was GNR No 172. Like contemporary British mainline stock, GNR carriages were of timber construction. The move from old style panelling to steel sheeting was made in 1935. The two K[15] Open Thirds seen either side of N382 were a direct development of the centre corridor design in the previous picture.

AG Cramp/Colour-Rail

Although GNR hauled stock had the mahogany livery, buses, diesel railcars and multiple unit diesel trains carried a more modern scheme of Oxford blue and cream. However, AEC-fitted trailers often found their way onto steam trains, creating rakes of mixed livery. In 1953 the joint UTA/GNR Royal Train was also painted blue and cream (by the UTA at York Road), resulting in six other vehicles running in this livery in the years following – two C^2 Firsts, two D^5 Brake/Firsts, a B^4 Dining Car and this A^5 Directors' Saloon, No 50, built in 1911 and seen at Belfast about 1958. This served as the Royal Saloon in 1953 and is preserved by the RPSI at Whitehead.

Reg Ludgate/Colour-Rail

Modern GNR catering stock is represented by B^9 Buffet Car No 124, seen at Strabane as part of a BUT formation on 2 August 1958. Like the Dining Cars used on some Dublin trains it is end kitchen in layout. No 124 was built in 1942 and served mainly tea, light snacks and the usual stronger refreshments. It eventually became UTA No 553 and was not scrapped until 1971, though out of use since early 1965. Note how the railcar livery was carried round the ends of the coach by Dundalk, whereas No 50, painted by the UTA, has black ends.

ES Russell/Colour-Rail

On the same train at Strabane we see K^{15} Open Third No 176. The carriage destination board would today fall foul of the Trade Descriptions Act! The K^{15} was the most numerous class of GNR coach, with 30 built in 1935–48. Half of them, including No 176, were conversions from wartime utility coaches built in 1942–43. The K^{15} was a modern development of the centre corridor Third seen on page 23. The design was unusual among open thirds in having four doors each side, a feature that later made them very popular for enthusiast specials where a rapid exit at photo stops had advantages!

ES Russell/Colour-Rail

BUSES

Although we tend to think of the GNR as a railway, it saw itself as a transport provider in a wider sense and in the 1950s had a fleet of about 160 buses and 100 lorries, not to mention an electric tram fleet. Up to 1935, the GNR operated buses on both sides of the border but the formation of the Northern Ireland Road Transport Board in that year forced it to concentrate its road-based activities south of the border, apart from some cross-border services. Within the Irish Free State (Irish Republic from 1949) it had an arrangement with CIÉ which gave it a monopoly of road services roughly corresponding to its railway operating area, including urban bus services on the north side of Dublin. Brought up in a part of Northern Ireland where they did not operate, I had little awareness of GNR buses as a child, except for occasional sightings at Enniskillen.

We start our bus section with a view of No 321 in the Market Yard at Ballyshannon on 7 July 1959. Ballyshannon was on the Bundoran branch which had closed in September 1957. No 321 was very typical of GNR buses – a Gardner-engined vehicle built at Dundalk. She was built in 1941 but was rebodied again in 1950 in this attractive 'Windover' style with very distinctive windows. Although owned by CIÉ in this photograph, No 321 has yet to be renumbered G321 or receive CIÉ colours. It was withdrawn in 1962.

David Soggee

Ex-GNR AEC Regal III No 415 at Broadstone, Dublin on 2 September 1967. This was one of a batch of 30 Regal IIIs bodied by Park Royal and delivered to the GNR in the summer and autumn of 1948. Nos 403–26 were 39 seaters and, until the first Royal Tigers arrived in 1952, were the largest capacity single deckers on the GNR. Nos 427–32 were given 35 coach seats for tour work. GNR half cab single deckers usually had the canopy cut back over the nearside front. Most of these Regal IIIs were withdrawn in the mid 1960s but this one survived until 1971.

Richard Whitford

GNR double-deckers were sourced from AEC and were much in evidence on North Dublin suburban services. The earliest were ten Regent Is purchased in 1937 but this is one from the post-war batches of Regent IIIs. Some of these double-deckers had platform doors for operating rural services, including Dundalk–Newry, making the GNR one of only a handful of bus companies worldwide to operate double-deckers across an international boundary. No 438 was built in 1948, was withdrawn in 1967 and is now preserved. It is seen at Dundalk about 1958. The location is Hughes Park and the GNR ran a service from there to Quay Street to accommodate people working in the various factories. *Photobus*

In 1952 the GNR purchased its first underfloor-engined buses in the shape of a batch of four Saunders Roe-bodied Royal Tigers (Nos 225–28). These had an unusual centre entrance and seated 44. No 225, still in GNR livery, was photographed on the ramp at Amiens Street station on 18 July 1961, with the GNR crest painted out. It was withdrawn in 1972.
Richard Whitford

The Royal Tigers were followed by several batches of similar styled AEC Regal IVs in 1954–56. However, these were Park Royal-bodied with more conventional rear entrances. A total of 33 were built (Nos 260–76 and Nos 331–46) – 16 as 45-seat buses, four as 35-seat coaches and 13 as 40-seat dual-purpose vehicles. Most had IY or ZY Dublin registrations, but bus-bodied No 271, seen here at Donegal on 18 May 1958, uniquely had a Belfast registration. All these vehicles were later rebuilt by CIÉ with front entrances and lasted to the early 1970s.
JG Dewing

BELFAST

Now that we have surveyed the main elements of the GNR fleet, it is appropriate to take a geographical tour of the GNR railway network. I propose to look firstly at the services which commenced at Belfast and then later in the book at those originating in Dublin, concluding with a look at the Irish North.

The GNR terminus in Belfast was at Great Victoria Street, very close to the city centre, and was a very well-known landmark before its demolition in 1976 to make way for the Europa Hotel. Although this September 1964 view is slightly outside our period, it captures the atmosphere outside the station very well. The porte cochere, added in 1891, was originally intended for those in carriages to mount and dismount in comfort.   *David Soggee*

This view was taken inside the terminus looking out towards Great Victoria Street. This entrance enabled taxis to come right into the station and its position can be identified by the BEA advertisement in the previous picture. Platforms 1–4 are immediately to the right of the photographer and Platform 5 behind. Today this area is absorbed into the Europa Bus Centre. Thankfully, realising the remoteness of Central Station from the city centre, NIR decided to return to this site for a downtown station in 1995, though, sadly, without the imposing facade. Robinson's bar, across the street, is still a Belfast landmark.   *Derek Young*

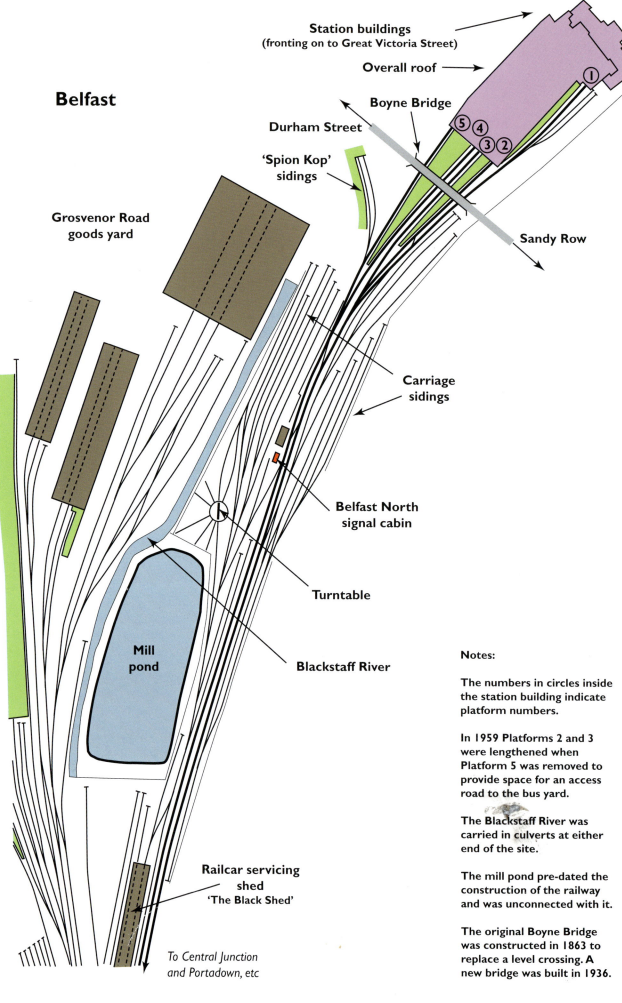

Belfast

Station buildings
(fronting on to Great Victoria Street)

Overall roof

Boyne Bridge

Durham Street

'Spion Kop' sidings

Grosvenor Road goods yard

Sandy Row

Carriage sidings

Belfast North signal cabin

Turntable

Mill pond

Blackstaff River

Railcar servicing shed 'The Black Shed'

To Central Junction and Portadown, etc

Notes:

The numbers in circles inside the station building indicate platform numbers.

In 1959 Platforms 2 and 3 were lengthened when Platform 5 was removed to provide space for an access road to the bus yard.

The Blackstaff River was carried in culverts at either end of the site.

The mill pond pre-dated the construction of the railway and was unconnected with it.

The original Boyne Bridge was constructed in 1863 to replace a level crossing. A new bridge was built in 1936.

This is the business end of Great Victoria Street in August 1956. Although 1956 was a generally good summer, this day was clearly not one of the best. Qs 4-4-0 No 121 makes a spirited departure from Platform 3 on a Derry line train, with a B¹ Dining Car at the head. At Platform 4, a PPs 4-4-0 shunts an AEC railcar. The two sidings just to the left of the engine were known as the 'Spion Kop', a name with Boer War connotations. They turned in sharply at about 50° and were used for vans to and from the cross-channel boats. In the centre, the dome of Belfast City Hall towers above the rooftops, whilst to the left is the tower of Church House.

Keith Pirt

On 19 October 1957, a three-car AEC set leaves from Platform 1. This short platform, just visible behind the rear car, was used for suburban services to Lisburn and Portadown and was known as the 'motor platform' because of its earlier use by railmotors in 1905–13. The centre car in this and three other AEC diesel trains was a K²³ Buffet Car but the buffet was small and could be locked up if the set was on suburban duties. Murray's Tobacco Factory dominated the south side of the station; although the building is still there in 2005, the business is due for closure. It accounted for the peculiar musty/sweet smell associated with the site. The Boyne Bridge, over the station, also visible in the previous picture, carried Durham Street and was built in Ulster Railway days to replace a level crossing.

WE Robertson/Colour-Rail

On a somewhat better day, and from the same vantage point, VS 4-4-0 No 209 *Foyle* prepares to depart from Platform 4 with (possibly) the 3.00pm to Dublin, about 1958. This picture gives a clearer view of Platform 5, seen earlier. With regular departures for destinations such as Newcastle, Antrim, Newry and Clones, as well as those mentioned earlier, five platforms were kept very busy but there was no room for expansion. After the closure of the Armagh and Newcastle lines had reduced traffic, the UTA removed Platform 5 in 1959, so that buses could use the trackbed as an access road to Glengall Street yard. *Reg Ludgate/Colour-Rail*

Looking in the opposite direction, we see S2 class 4-4-0 No 190 *Lugnaquilla* arriving at Platform 4 with the 9.00am from Dublin. This superb view was taken in May 1947 and is one of the earliest surviving colour pictures of the GNR. The photographer is standing on Platform 3 and his perspective takes in the extensive carriage sidings to the north of the station approaches. The errand boy with his bicycle adds to the atmosphere. The GNR employed lower quadrant signals throughout. Each signal seen here has a smaller 'calling on' arm for shunting movements.

AD Hutchinson/Colour-Rail

In this view, on 10 July 1959, the photographer is in the same position but has turned round to record the arrival of U class 4-4-0 No 196 *Lough Gill* at Platform 4. The engine has just been renumbered 64 by the UTA – note the crude painting out of the GNR crest and lettering. On shunting duty is T2 4-4-2T No 5,

a type commonly used for station pilot duties up to about 1961. Typical of the 1950s is the Royal Mail Trojan van parked on what was Platform 5, but the track has already disappeared.

David Soggee

It is July 1956 and VS 4-4-0 No 210 *Erne* is departing with a heavy Dublin express. The normal modern rake has been strengthened at the front by an older centre corridor Third. Behind it is an L¹⁴ Brake/Third, a C² all First and B⁴ Dining Car No 403, built in 1951 and still in its Royal Train livery. To the left of the engine

is Belfast's busy North Cabin, which controlled the station approaches out to Central Junction, half a mile away, and No 399, one of the two GNR Kitchen Cars. Note the tall water tank adjacent to the 'Spion Kop' and used mainly for watering carriages.

Keith Pirt

In another scene at the same location, Qs 4-4-0 No 131 shunts a two car AEC railcar set on 19 October 1957. This shows one of the AEC 'mules' or 'Doodlebugs' coupled to the engine. These were non-powered AEC driving trailers, two of which (Nos 8 and 9) were built in 1954. Their main function was to allow a single railcar to continue operating if its 'partner' was under repair. No 9 is preserved by the RPSI, albeit without its driving cab. To the left is coach No 474, an ex-LNWR side corridor Third, one of several purchased from the LMS in 1947. It was built in 1907 and had been LMS No 3474. *WE Robertson/Colour-Rail*

Another of Belfast's 4-4-2Ts pauses between shunting duties on 23 November 1961. No 187 was the last of the T1 class and was to stagger on for another couple of years. The station is out of sight to the right of this view. Behind the engine is an area of water known as 'the duck pond'. It was the water supply to a linen mill and pre-dated the railway. Beyond it is Grosvenor Road goods yard, which was the main GNR freight terminal in Belfast, Adelaide being only a marshalling yard. The yard and 'the pond' are nowadays under the Westlink dual carriageway.

Des FitzGerald

In the goods yard itself, but four years earlier, on 19 October 1957, LQGs 0-6-0 No 163 is engaged in shunting close to the extensive goods sheds, out of sight to the right. The GNR had a very considerable goods traffic, as virtually all cross-border freight had to use its metals. South of the border, GNR lorries picked up and delivered rail-borne goods, but north of the border all road freight was in the hands of the UTA, this being the work my father was involved in. His office in Portadown was just beside the GNR goods yard there. This particular LQGs went to CIÉ in 1958 and was withdrawn at the end of 1962.
WE Robertson/Colour-Rail

Moving slightly closer to the goods sheds, now visible on the right, SG2 0-6-0 No 184 has arrived at Grosvenor Road with some seven-plank open wagons on the same day. The GNR made extensive use of full and half-sized containers and in the right distance a half container can be seen in an open wagon. As most goods trains ran at night, the GNR used a lot of 0-6-0s for shunting during the day. Access to Grosvenor Road was controlled from Central Junction cabin.
WE Robertson/Colour-Rail

The extensive GNR network in Belfast included the Belfast Central Railway with its access to the docks and the BCDR in East Belfast. The RT 0-6-4Ts, described earlier, were built for shunting these lines and the last of the type was No 166, seen here as UTA No 24 on 12 May 1962. Note the total lack of styling in the bunker. This view is at Maysfields, below East Bridge Street, precisely where the modern railway enters Central Station. In the 1950s and early 1960s, Maysfields handled all the cattle traffic that originated in Tyrone, Fermanagh, Cavan, Leitrim and beyond.
CCQ1848/Des FitzGerald collection

The same engine is seen shunting at Donegall Quay two years earlier, in May 1960. The dock lines seen here were accessed by a line which ran north from East Bridge Junction along the west bank of the Lagan and through a restricted tunnel (The Queen's Bridge Subway), passing under the Queen's Bridge, near the north end of Oxford Street. From there the lines fanned out round the docks and had a link to the NCC system at York Road. This view is at the Ardrossan terminal and the mast of the Ardrossan steamer is evident. The Subway required cut-down boiler mountings, less obvious on these engines because of their low slung boilers, but the covered wagon shows how small the engine is.

JG Dewing/Colour-Rail IR598

On 12 May 1962, PGs 0-6-0 No 10 is traversing Donegall Quay with a train of cattle wagons and British Railways containers in open wagons. This cobbled road was also used by road traffic, explaining the railway porter with the red flag. By 1962, No 10 was the last survivor of the PGs class.

Des FitzGerald

ADELAIDE

The Belfast locomotive shed was located a mile from Great Victoria Street, at Adelaide, where the GNR also had its marshalling yard. As a kid, my eyes were usually glued to the window from here into Belfast, as steam engines were to be seen at the shunting yard, the shed and, closer to Belfast, Grosvenor Road. Adelaide shed was a rectangular affair with nine parallel roads orientated northeast-southwest, able to accomodate 55 locomotives inside and many more outside. Unusually for such a large shed, there was no turntable, engines being turned on a large triangle in the bog meadow. Engines did not have to use the busy double track main line to get to and from Great Victoria Street as there was a 'third road' used only by goods trains and light engines. Sections of this still survive today. The present, sadly redundant, Adelaide goods yard occupies part of the site. The rest is under the adjacent industrial estate.

Views looking into the shed are rare because the sun was usually in the wrong direction, but this March 1959 picture gives a glimpse of the building with its hinged wooden doors. Inside, and unusually facing out, are VS class 4-4-0 No 210 *Erne* and V class 4-4-0 compound No 86 *Peregrine*. Most Adelaide engines were turned after servicing so that they were chimney towards Dublin as they reversed to the terminal for their next duty. However, these two were not in steam because it was a Sunday.
Alan Chandler/Colour-Rail

Late afternoon photographs were particularly difficult at Adelaide on sunny days as the best photographic vantage point was facing west, as here. It is May 1957 and S class 4-4-0 No 173 *Galteemore* is ready for duty in the more normal posture of chimney towards the shed, as is the Compound alongside, probably No 84 which had this unique firebox. Note the staff-catching equipment on the tender, a feature of engines used on the single track Derry Road.
Colour-Rail IR176

By 4 April 1960, two GNR compounds together was a rare sight. Here, the last UTA example, No 86 *Peregrine*, rests alongside the last CIÉ example, No 85 *Merlin*, which is on a day excursion from Dublin. *Des FitzGerald*

Oddly, the GNR never modernised any of its sheds with mechanical coal chutes, such as those the NCC installed at York Road and Coleraine. At most sheds coal was laboriously shovelled directly from wagons by hand. At Adelaide there was an elevated coaling stage. Wagons of coal were shunted up an inclined plane to the level of the brickwork and tipped into the engines below. In September 1956, VS class 4-4-0 No 206 *Liffey* waits its turn at the ramp. Engines also took water at this point and the fireman waits for the 4000 gallon tender to fill. I remember Portadown driver Fred Moore giving me a footplate trip round to the coaling stage to witness this when I was in my teens.

JG Wallace/Colour-Rail

This view dates from 1964, in UTA days, but shows the layout of the coaling stage, the ramp and approach road. By this date the roof was in very bad condition. Like many engine sheds, Adelaide could be a muddy and dirty environment, especially in the winter months. The original arches in the approach ramp have been bricked up to provide stores.

Derek Young

This interesting view, on 1 August 1959, shows QLs class 4-4-0 No 156 on the Adelaide turning triangle (out of shot to the left). On the right is the rear of the engine shed, with two old six-wheeled coaches. Note also the ex-NCC U2 class 4-4-0, to the right of No 156, stored for scrapping. The south end of the coaling stage is visible just above the tender, with an engine taking coal. It is not totally clear what is happening here, as No 156 is already coaled and turned. The normal procedure was for engines to take coal while still facing Belfast and then move onto the triangle.

ES Russell/Colour-Rail

BELFAST TO PORTADOWN
AND THE ANTRIM BRANCH

All GNR trains out of Belfast followed the same route as far as Lisburn and Knockmore Junction, so this was a very busy stretch of line with trains every few minutes. I had my first opportunity to observe this in person in the early months of 1957 when I had a spell in Musgrave Park Hospital, two miles from Belfast. My ward was close to the line and the cavalcade of trains provided endless fascination and variety.

A delightful view of U class 4-4-0 No 202 *Louth* passing through Finaghy on Wednesday 6 May 1959. Finaghy was the third station out of Belfast. Although built for the Irish North, the U class were redeployed to other routes after those lines closed in 1957. This is a train from Antrim and is almost certainly the 7.25am, then the only weekday steam-operated service on the branch. No 202 is probably within days of being renumbered 67 by the UTA.

JG Dewing/Colour-Rail IR491

This deceptively rural scene is near Derriaghy, the fifth suburban station out of Belfast. Today it would be a lot more built up. Approaching in the down direction (ie from Dublin), on Saturday 9 July 1960, is VS 4-4-0 No 207 *Boyne*, then in CIÉ ownership. The train is probably a day excursion from Dublin, comprising older GNR panelled coaches. No 207 was sold to the UTA in June 1963 and was destined to be the last of the class.

Des FitzGerald

Lisburn station on 6 May 1959. This is a morning view and the AEC railcar at Platform 1 is probably the 10.15am local to Belfast. Forty six years on, the track layout at the Belfast end of Lisburn is little changed. Note the track ganger walking along the No 2 Platform road, with his hammer for striking loose keys. The track trailing off to the right right ran to a small loco turntable. Bicycle sheds, like those on Platform 1, were once a common feature of railway stations. *JG Dewing*

Today Lisburn has the status of a city and has one of the best preserved brick-built GNR stations I have seen. This view is at the Dublin end of the station on Friday 15 May 1959. U class 4-4-0 No 200 *Lough Melvin* has a local train, possibly for Newry. Although I have heard these Us with traditional cab cut-outs described as 'proper Us', my personal favourites were the 1948 batch with cab windows and higher-pitched boilers.

R Denison/Colour-Rail

A mile and a half beyond Lisburn was Knockmore Junction, where two branches diverged to Newcastle and Antrim. Sadly, no colour is available of the line to Banbridge and Newcastle, which closed in 1955 beyond Banbridge and entirely in 1956. The Antrim branch remained open to passengers until 1960 but did not close entirely and was reopened by NIR in more recent times. Today it is once again closed, but time will tell! Here a UG 0-6-0 pauses at Ballinderry and the signalman gives the driver a friendly wave. My Grandfather was stationmaster at nearby Brookmount in the years before World War One.

John Langford

The same train approaches Glenavy. Notice the small goods yard on the up side. The engine in shadow is probably UG 0-6-0 No 82. My first and only run over this line in a service train, before closure in 1960, was on Saturday 4 July 1959 when I travelled on the 1.10pm working, which, from recollection, was also hauled by a UG.

John Langford

On 16 May 1960, John Dewing travelled on the 5.43pm service train from Belfast, joining it at Hilden and enjoying a footplate trip from Lisburn. The engine on this service returned at 8.35pm on the goods and the carriage set worked back as the 7.25am the following day, using the engine from the overnight 2.30am goods. On this occasion the engine was U class 4-4-0 No 196 *Lough Gill* (by then UTA No 64). This view is at Aldergrove where Great-Grandfather Johnston was stationmaster in the late 19th century. He may even have been the first as the line only opened in 1871. *JG Dewing*

Lough Gill has arrived at the Great Northern bay at Antrim with its five coach rake, the second of which is an ex-NCC Compartment Third of LMS origin. The crew wait for John Dewing to take his shot before moving onto the turntable. After turning, the engine will work back to Belfast on the goods at 8.35pm and the carriages will stay here until the following morning's 7.25am to Belfast. Unusually, No 196 has a 3500 gallon D1 type tender from one of the S class engines, probably for working Bangor to Dublin excursions. *JG Dewing*

Returning to the main line, we continue towards Portadown with this Sunday morning view of an up train at Moira on 3 April 1960. The engine is again U 4-4-0 No 202, though by this date both engine and carriages carry UTA numbers. The train is very probably an excursion for Warrenpoint and is about to cross the Lagan Canal. The plate on the white-painted post indicated the bridge number, starting from 0 at Dublin. The two GNR-liveried coaches are K8 centre corridor Thirds dating from 1915, whilst the green one is a later K11. *Des FitzGerald*

PORTADOWN

Although Lurgan is a major station, no one seems to have taken colour pictures in GNR days, so we move reluctantly on to Portadown (Sorry, Lurgan!). I spent my formative years in Portadown and saw it gradually transformed from a busy three-way junction to a suburban outpost on NIR's main line to Dublin. Portadown was the only three-way junction in Ireland where all routes were double track. It had a very busy goods yard, as goods trains arriving from all four routes were remarshalled and dispatched in different directions. Most goods departures took place in the early hours of the morning, so my sleep was usually against a background of whistling and heavy starts, but I wasn't complaining!

We start our coverage of Portadown at the Boilie level crossing and block post, between Lurgan and Portadown, on 1 August 1959. QLs class 4-4-0 No 156 heads the 4.55pm Belfast–Londonderry. This photograph was taken on the same day as the earlier view at Adelaide (on page 37) and this was the service it was being prepared for. By this date No 156 was the last operational QLs and was scrapped the following March. Today the land on either side of this picture is occupied by the 'Balancing Lakes' at Craigavon.

ES Russell/Colour-Rail

Closer to Portadown, we see Qs class 4-4-0 No 134 at McCaughey's Bridge in May 1947, on what is probably a Clones train. This is another very early GNR colour scene and must have been quite a challenge to capture as it is of a moving train. Of particular note is that this engine was the first Qs to be withdrawn and went as early as December 1951, so this is probably the only colour picture ever taken of it.

AD Hutchinson/Colour-Rail IR567

Viewed from Portadown's North Cabin, U class 4-4-0 No 198 *Lough Swilly* arrives in from Belfast on 28 May 1957, proving that not all U class engines were on the Irish North in GNR days. The road is set for Platform 1, which was on the town side. The cabin was at the end of the island platform, and the crossover in the foreground allowed vans to be shunted from Platform 3 to Platform 2 without blocking access to or from Platform 1. The vans were usually 'Free to Free' traffic – Dublin to Strabane for Donegal and vice versa. In the left background are the carriage sidings. Down direction trains faced a stiff climb up to Seagoe, on the horizon.

AD Hutchinson/Colour-Rail

Portadown

River Bann

South cabin

Water tower

Station building

North cabin

To Lurgan

On Thursday 8 July 1948 an absolutely pristine No 83 *Eagle* enters Portadown with the 12.00 noon for Dublin. At this date Nos 84 and 87 had already been rebuilt with Belpaire fireboxes and No 86 was in hand, so it is rare to have a colour shot of a Compound with the original round topped firebox. The normal seven coach rake has been strengthened by two more at the front. Two railwaymen wait beside the North cabin to cross on the barrow walk, whilst in the distance a down train climbs Seagoe bank.

AD Hutchinson/
Colour-Rail IR561

A few minutes later, No 83 waits at the south end of Platform 2 ready to depart for Dublin. Note the permanently-fitted 'Enterprise' nameboard fitted to many of the big engines. These were simply swung down when the train was not the 'Enterprise'. Water cranes were conveniently located at the south end of Platforms 1 and 2 and the north end of 3 and 4. In the background is Platform 4, which is the only part of the station to survive today, as it is part of a Northern Ireland Railways permanent way depot.

AD Hutchinson/
Colour-Rail IR562

On Thursday 3 June 1948, S class 4-4-0 No 170 *Errigal* waits at the south end of Platform 3, perhaps to detach a van from the rear of the Derry–Belfast train behind it. At Platform 4 is the rear of a train from Clones or Warrenpoint and at Platform 2 is a K[15] Third on a Dublin train. The white boards on the rear of trains were used to indicate 'end of train' for signalmen. A train passing without this board indicated a runaway.

AD Hutchinson/
Colour-Rail IR568

In July 1953, U class 4-4-0 No 200 *Lough Melvin* departs from Platform 1 with a good head of steam and carrying the correct 'ordinary passenger train' headlamp code. This is probably a train for Newry, the composition being a D² Brake/First, an F¹⁶ Composite and two Corridor Thirds. Behind the train, another engine is blowing off in the short 'Bann siding', used mainly by pilot engines or engines waiting to replace another. To the right, is the yard of Portadown Foundry and the train is about to cross the Bann bridge. *AD Hutchinson/Colour-Rail IR571*

Beyond the goods yard, Portadown shed was tucked into the gap at the junction between the Dublin and Clones lines. Portadown had a concrete roundhouse and in this August 1959 view No 173 *Galteemore* is on the turntable. The Clones line can just be seen above the front buffer, whilst beyond it the goods train marks the position of the Derry Road. This whole area has changed beyond recognition today and the roundabout where the Armagh and Dungannon roads now diverge is roughly the area behind the engine here. The shed stoutly resisted attempts to demolish it in 1970 and explosives had to be resorted to! *Keith Pirt*

U class 4-4-0 No 198 *Lough Swilly* makes a stirring sight as it passes under the Armagh Road bridge and past the site of the former Tavanagh signal cabin (left of the train) on the outskirts of Portadown in May 1957. The engine is on the main line, heading for Warrenpoint and, as well as the usual four coaches, has two vans in tow. In my teens, I was a regular visitor to the house marked by the tree on the far side of the bridge and did a lot of my train spotting from the garden there.

AD Hutchinson/Colour-Rail

An AEC diesel railcar, on a southbound working, approaches Knock Bridge, a few miles south of Portadown, in June 1951. This is the earliest colour slide I have come across of one of these trains and the presence of a K^{23} Buffet Car and destination board suggests that this is an 'Enterprise' working, probably the 4.45pm return working of the Dublin-based set. The buffet car staff had an interesting problem with an ingenious solution. The excise duty on drink differed on each side of the border so, to keep things legal, there were two drinks cabinets of the same size and a lockable door was taken from one and placed over the other on crossing the border!

AD Hutchinson/Colour-Rail

A nicely composed shot at the same location in July 1953. (The diesel above was photographed from the bridge in the background.) The engine is QGs 0-6-0 No 153 and, as this class was associated with the Banbridge lines, it is just possible that the train is going from Portadown to Banbridge via Scarva. Certainly the headlamp code indicates a slow, stopping goods.

AD Hutchinson/Colour-Rail

GORAGHWOOD TO WARRENPOINT

One important landmark on the Dublin line was Goraghwood, where the Armagh–Warrenpoint line made a junction with the main line. In the 1950s the section to Newry and Warrenpoint remained very busy but the Armagh line had been reduced to a goods only branch from Goraghwood to Markethill.

Goraghwood cabin was at the south end of the up platform, which was an island, Warrenpoint trains using the far side. On 10 September 1960 VS 4-4-0 No 208 *Lagan* (now No 58) pauses on its way south with a CIÉ-liveried set on the 3.15pm up. At this time carriage sets worked through to Belfast and Dublin but engines were changed at Dundalk. A goods train lies over in the background. Goods trains were usually halted at Goraghwood for Customs inspection and for the removal or addition of Newry wagons.

Des FitzGerald

On 15 May 1959, Gardner Railcar F departs from Goraghwood with the shuttle to Newry. These railcars connected with all main line trains to provide a local service but in addition several trains went right through to Belfast (see page 18). The view of the Dublin line is blocked by the cabin but it climbed steeply from this point, whereas the branch dropped in like manner. Viewed from a departing Dublin train, the branch set could often be seen away below but not that far distant.

R Denison/Colour-Rail

A very good shot of Railcar F as it heads south from the junction with an afternoon train in May 1959, quite possibly on the same date as the view earlier. The main line is on the embankment to the left. From here it was 3½ miles to Newry. This section was opened by the Newry and Armagh Railway in 1854 and became part of the GNR in 1879. The Warrenpoint line was built by the Newry, Warrenpoint and Rostrevor Railway in 1849 and remained independent until 1886. Despite its name, it never reached Rostrevor. The left-hand track was at one time the access to the railbus turntable. *Chris Gammell/Colour-Rail IR517*

The main station in Newry was Edward Street and this view was taken in August 1963. In the summer the up line was in use for through trains. Although taken in 1963 this is almost an authentic GNR scene. The engine is the now-preserved No 171 *Slieve Gullion* and at this angle it is impossible to see the carriage livery! The notice on the right still claims that the station is served by trains for Armagh; even via Portadown this had no longer been true for six years. The roof had strong similarities to that at Armagh. The advertising hoardings behind the far platform seat proclaimed LMS ownership, but updating its property at Newry was hardly a priority for British Railways, even after 15 years! *David Soggee*

Newry (Edward Street)

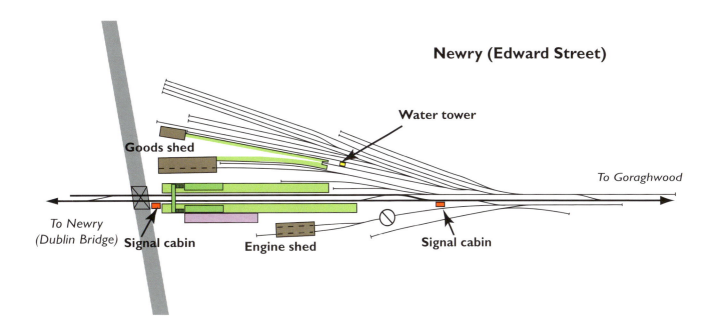

This wintry view shows the south end of Newry Edward Street on Monday 28 December 1964, a week before it closed. Each winter the right-hand track was turned into a siding. The photographer is standing on Edward Street level crossing. One of the factors which in the end doomed the branch was the large number of level crossings in the town (five within about half a mile), creating a situation rather like that at Hull. The footbridge was very typically Great Northern.
WFM Wallace

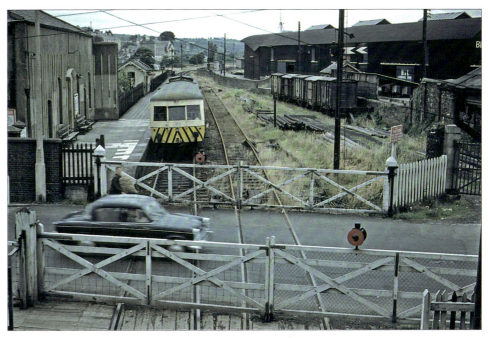

Newry Dublin Bridge station, looking towards Warrenpoint on Friday 28 July 1961. This was not the original terminus of the NWRR, which was at Kilmorey Street to the left. This station was built when the two Newry lines were connected in 1861. In the foreground a Singer Gazelle passes on William Street and Railcar F is at the platform. Behind the photographer was the Newry Canal and Buttercrane Quay. The line from Edward Street passed through what is now the Buttercrane Shopping Centre.
WFM Wallace

Warrenpoint was a busy station, serving the port of Warrenpoint and attracting a lot of excursion traffic, particularly on Sundays when a short boat trip to Omeath in the Republic enabled drinkers to bypass Northern Ireland's strict licensing laws. Like a number of GNR termini, Warrenpoint station had a train shed. On 4 July 1961, U class 4-4-0 No 200 *Lough Melvin* has just arrived from Goraghwood. We have a good view of the corridor side of a K13 Third.

Des FitzGerald

This interesting view shows passengers queueing to have their tickets checked as they leave a train at Warrenpoint in September 1964. Notice the very typical yellow brickwork, with black and purple courses, which was a feature of so many GNR stations. The view is looking back towards Newry. The Northern Ireland Government in the 1950s was keen to develop the Port of Warrenpoint and several road-widening schemes of the time were part of that plan. Thus the A4 and A5 roads from Fermanagh and Tyrone were widened as far as Ballygawley, followed by Aughnacloy–Armagh and Armagh–Newry but not Ballygawley to Belfast.

David Soggee

PORTADOWN TO CLONES

Although I was a regular traveller on this line in the 1950s, I was too young to wield a camera in those far off days. For some reason no one seems to have taken colour slides of this line, though it is adequately covered in black and white. The only view I have seen is an already published scene at Tynan. In order to show anything at all of this important line, I have had to fall back on post-closure views.

We start with a colour shot of the lifting train at Stone Bridge in 1959. The engine is SG3 0-6-0 No 49, running as UTA No 36, but still in GNR livery and is heading in the Portadown direction. The Portadown–Clones line closed on 30 September 1957, the same day as the Irish North and Bundoran branch. However, the UTA lifted the Glaslough–Portadown section in 1958–59, before the Irish North which went in 1959–62. Stone Bridge is about three-quarters of the way between Portadown and Richhill.
Des FitzGerald

The first station on the line was Richhill, which was a very considerable distance from the village it served. This was what the station looked like on 27 April 1962, in a view looking back towards Portadown. Note how the rails embedded in the road have been left in situ and indeed tarmaced over. Although the level crossing gates are gone, the pillars remain. Today, this scene is not much changed and the station is now a private house.
Des FitzGerald

Armagh station in February 1963, not long before it was completely demolished. The station building was designed by Sir John MacNeill and bears a close resemblance to his stations at Portadown and Monaghan; only Monaghan remains today. A common feature of all three was the grand entrance porch. Armagh station is now the Ulsterbus depot and garage (not the bus station) and the elaborate and attractive gates still survive, as does the enormous goods store. Armagh is a city and, when the line was opened in 1848, Belfast was not. The locals took great delight in pointing out that the Ulster Railway connected the *City* of Armagh to the *town* of Belfast! Armagh was itself the junction for two branch lines, to Newry and to Castleblayney (see page 99). The section of the Newry line from Armagh to Markethill closed in 1933 and was the line on which the major accident had occurred in 1889; Markethill–Newry remained open for goods after 1933 and finally closed in 1955. *Des FitzGerald*

The Castleblayney branch opened from Armagh as far as Keady in 1908 (for goods only until 1909) and throughout in 1910. Partition in 1921 killed traffic on the line and it closed beyond Keady in 1923. In the 1950s the Armagh–Keady section was still operating, though it had been a goods only line since 1932. It closed on the same day as the Clones line – 30 September 1957. This is Keady station on 24 December 1961, after the line was lifted. We are looking towards Armagh and the layout of the run round loop can still be discerned. *Des FitzGerald*

Below the signal cabin at Keady was this interesting tunnel, photographed on the same date. When the line was opened in 1908 there were plans to build a narrow gauge railway (the Ulster and Connaught Light Railway) linking Newry with the Cavan and Leitrim Railway via Bessbrook, Keady and the Clogher Valley. This bridge was built to accomodate the proposed line, which was not in fact built. Today the bridge is bricked up at the far end and is used as a bus garage, giving Ulsterbus, Keady, a unique bit of infrastructure.

Des FitzGerald

Returning to the Armagh–Clones line, the first station out of Armagh was Killylea, seen here on 31 December 1962. This was another completely rural station and, like Richhill, very remote from its village. We are looking towards Tynan in this view and the sleeper indentations suggest that only the up platform had been in use latterly. This tranquil scene has changed little today, the present owner having preserved the platforms, buildings and even the signal cabin.

Des FitzGerald

An early morning view of Tynan on 31 December 1962, looking towards Armagh. Apart from the weeds, not much deterioration has taken place at Tynan since the tracks were lifted four years earlier. The cabin was still glazed. Tynan was a Customs Post on the line to Monaghan and Clones. Despite its importance, photographers seem to also have ignored Monaghan, perhaps because trains did not terminate there.

Des FitzGerald

PORTADOWN TO OMAGH

We now move to the third route out of Portadown, the much-lamented 'Derry Road' with its fierce gradients and varied scenery. Coverage of intermediate stations in colour is patchy, but in any case there is not room to show them all. In many cases 'out of the window' shots in UTA days will have to suffice, as little else is available.

Trew and Moy was the third station from Portadown on the Derry Road, the first two being Annaghmore and Verner's Bridge. Trew was the townland in which the station stood but it really served the village of Moy, well-known for having had the largest horse fair in Western Europe in the eighteenth century. Despite the comparative importance of the two places, 'Moy and Trew' just doesn't have the right ring to it. This view on 11 August 1963 is looking towards Dungannon. This station now houses a mushroom packing business and the distant goods store has been tastefully restored as the works canteen. *John Langford*

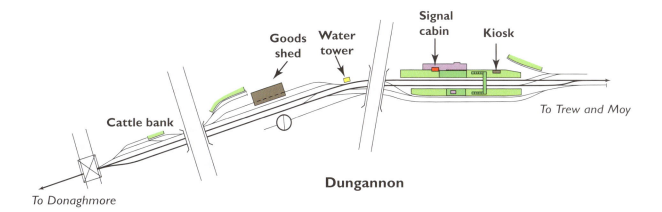

Goods shed

Water tower

Signal cabin

Kiosk

Cattle bank

To Trew and Moy

Dungannon

To Donaghmore

Opposite lower: Dungannon was the first major station on the line and this is the Portadown end in September 1959 with Qs 4-4-0 No 135 on a five coach Derry–Belfast train, probably a 'relief' or a Saturday extra. By 1959 the core service was operated by BUT railcars. The second coach is a railcar-fitted Buffet Car. The town lies to the right and was very close to the station. The fire surround in the waiting room beside the cabin declared 'Ulster Railway' and probably dated from 1858. The Qs class were the favourites for Derry line trains in steam days, because their relatively light frames were less rigid on this sharply twisting road.

McInnes/Des FitzGerald collection

Despite the popularity of the Qs class on this line, the S class began to make inroads from the mid-1950s. On 15 May 1956, No 173 *Galteemore* and the 5.00pm from Belfast provide a colourful scene, viewed from the road bridge at the Omagh end of the station. The engine carries the automatic staff exchange apparatus fitted to engines on this line. The leading carriage is one of those useful J[11] Tricomposite brakes, used by the GNR as through coaches. This vehicle was probably transferred from a Dublin–Belfast train at Portadown. *ES Russell/Colour-Rail*

About half a mile out of Dungannon a branch diverged to Cookstown, though it was closed to passengers in 1956 and became goods only. In 1959 the branch was truncated beyond Coalisland, this section only being retained because of Coalisland brickworks. This is the branch on 29 August 1964, showing the siding in Coalisland which branched off to the brickworks. The branch had several industrial sidings to collieries, sand pits and brickworks.
Derek Young

This is the imposing station at Coalisland on 11 August 1963, when the branch was still open but only the right-hand track was in use, though all is deceptively quiet here. We are looking towards Cookstown. The goods store is visible on the right and a track ran right through it, under the bridge beyond and then rejoined the main line to form a loop. Sand was another traffic which kept the branch open until 1965. In latter days, it was worked as a 5½ mile siding, by an engine which came to Dungannon every day from Portadown and worked back as a goods.
John Langford

It is hard to imagine nowadays that, before the Northern Ireland 'Troubles', troops were regularly moved from docks to barracks by train. This is just such a train leaving Pomeroy for Omagh on 11 October 1960. Today troops would be moved by helicopter and their stores by well-guarded road convoy. The motive power on this train is interesting – a U class 4-4-0 (No 202) piloting a T2 4-4-2T (No 30). Glover tanks were a rare sight on the Derry Road. Pomeroy was at the foot of the steepest bank on this line so this explains the pilot. The second coach is an F16 Corridor Composite.

Des FitzGerald

Having passed by Carrickmore, Sixmilecross and Beragh we reach Omagh, where the Derry Road merged with the 'Irish North'. On the Belfast side of Omagh was a short goods-only line, known as Omagh Market branch. The goods station here was used for traffic in the Belfast direction, whilst that at the main station served Enniskillen and Derry traffic, an odd arrangement dating back to 1861 and never changed by the GNR. Wagons were brought round here up to three times a day and this photograph was taken from the brake van of such a train on 20 July 1962, as the guard inserts the 'key' and switches the point for the branch. The wagons were then propelled down and shunted. Similarly, the return working involved propelling wagons from here to the station, ¾ mile away to the left. The new Omagh bypass road follows the main line cutting on the left.

Richard Whitford

Omagh Market goods station looks quite busy on the same day in this photograph of SG2 0-6-0 No 18 (UTA No 40) engaged in shunting. The fireman is trimming his coal during a pause in the operation. The large three-road goods store is in the distance and had two long platforms as well. The twin spires of the Sacred Heart church tower above. Today this site is occupied by the library headquarters and by part of Dunnes Stores. The young man is Derek Young; the low single storey building behind his head still survives.

Richard Whitford

Continuing round to Omagh passenger station, this is the view from the track looking towards Belfast on 19 March 1961. Trains at this end of Omagh were controlled from the South Cabin, now in UTA colours. On the right is the Irish North line to Enniskillen, so called because it was part of the Irish North Western Railway before the GNR was formed in 1876. The Irish North was still being lifted when this shot was taken and the right-hand track appears to be occupied by the brake van and wagons of the lifting train.

Des FitzGerald

In this view, the photographer is standing roughly where the wagons are in the previous photograph and looking back at the station. The up platform had the main building and was the longest platform at any GNR station. This had a short bay (just visible beyond the cabin) where vans were stored. The second goods yard is just visible through the canopy of the down platform.

JG Dewing

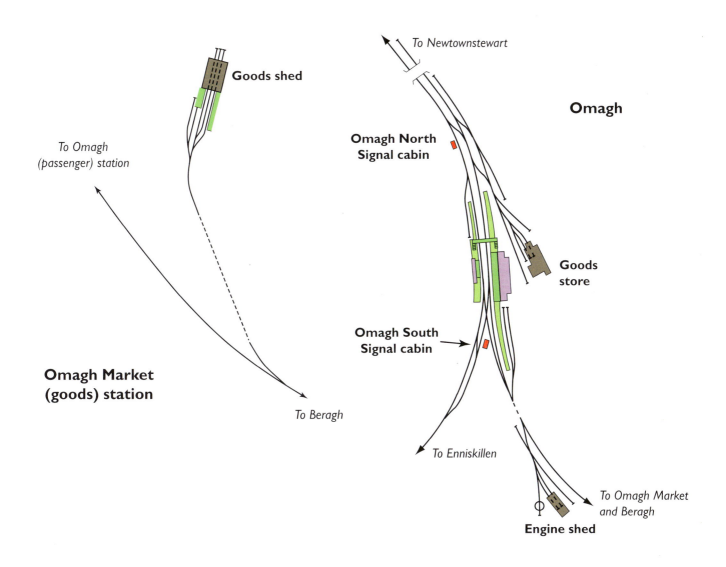

Goods shed

To Newtownstewart

Omagh

Omagh North Signal cabin

To Omagh (passenger) station

Omagh South Signal cabin

Goods store

Omagh Market (goods) station

To Beragh

To Enniskillen

To Omagh Market and Beragh

Engine shed

In 1958, railcar A was allocated to the UTA and was used for the rest of its revenue earning life on local services on the Derry Road. It was employed mainly between Derry and Strabane but one duty, the 6.08pm Strabane–Omagh, brought it to Omagh each day. Now renumbered 101, it sits at Omagh's up platform one afternoon in May 1960. In the left background we catch another glimpse of Omagh's other goods station.

JG Dewing/Colour-Rail IR493

FINTONA

We now diverge briefly down the Irish North to visit the famous Fintona branch, well known for being operated by the last horse tram in Ireland. At Fintona Junction, on Saturday 7 September 1957, an Enniskillen-bound train (probably the 10.40am) slows to a stop, hauled by PPs 4-4-0 No 12, built in 1911. The leading coach is another J[11] (see page 55). Note the fireman holding the staff. The up platform was an island, as seen in the next picture, and the tram used the other face. In 1993 I published a comprehensive history of the tram, my interest being sparked by the 25 years I lived in Omagh.

JM Chamney/Colour-Rail

Dick waits patiently at the Junction on the morning of Thursday 12 September 1957, while his driver, the redoubtable Willie McClean, chats to the guard of the Enniskillen train and the signalman and porter. The carriage is a non-corridor L[4] Brake/3rd. Normal procedure was for the tram to arrive ahead of the train, Dick would then be unhitched and walked to the small shed beside the cabin until the train had arrived. This was to avoid the steam engine scaring the horse.

Colin Hogg/Colour-Rail

On Friday 31 May 1957, locals take advantage of the lovely evening to travel on the upper deck of the tram up to the Junction and enjoy the view to the rear. We may speculate that the young man on the left is heading into Omagh for an evening of dancing.

The tram, numbered 381, and therefore in the carriage rather than the tram series, has just passed Liskey Cottage, in the centre background, while the terrace of houses to the right is on the Dromore Road. *FW Shuttleworth/Colour-Rail*

Fintona station on 8 May 1957. The tram terminated its 1100 yard journey in this covered train shed. 'Running round' was easier than with a steam engine! The houses in the background are on the main street, so Fintona was well served by the GNR. Note the soft grit, or cinder, path between the rails for Dick to walk on. The small stable is just to the left of the tram. The wagons remind us that steam engines came down the branch to work the extensive goods traffic. *Colour-Rail*

OMAGH TO STRABANE

Returning to the Derry Road, we now proceed in the Strabane direction. The first significant station on this section was Newtownstewart, about ten miles from Omagh. Between Omagh and there, the line followed the valley of the River Strule, crossing it at several points. This is Newtownstewart on 3 June 1963, the signalman having already collected the staff. The cabin was directly opposite on the up platform. A Ford Popular gives period atmosphere. The train is a BUT railcar and is probably the 3.00pm Belfast–Derry.   *Des FitzGerald*

On the same afternoon, the diesel train has stopped at Victoria Bridge, three and a half miles beyond Newtownstewart. The Nestlé factory on the right had its own siding and its car park has a lovely collection of classic cars, including Ford Anglias and Prefects, a 1957 Vaulhall Victor, a Rover P4, two Morris Minors and a Mini. Victoria Bridge was a tiny village but it was the railhead for Castlederg, seven miles distant and without trains since its steam tram ceased in 1933.   *Des FitzGerald*

A nice view of the rather unusual Victoria Bridge signal cabin, here painted in a rather more colourful fashion than it would have been before 1958. This was an afternoon train, making it difficult to photograph the down platform where the main buildings were situated. The station staff clearly have time for a bit of horticulture between duties. *Des FitzGerald*

The next station down the line was Sion Mills, less than two miles beyond Victoria Bridge. This picture illustrates a feature of many GNR stations, particularly on the Irish North, namely the station name displayed in large cast concrete letters where there was a suitable bank. This could be seen at Trillick, Enniskillen and Lisnaskea, to name but three. The only platform was on the down side and the stone and brick building was an 1883 replacement of an earlier structure. Opposite the station was Herdman's linen mill which provided much employment and featured in the 2004 BBC *Restoration* programme.

Des FitzGerald

STRABANE

We now come to the major junction of Strabane where, until 1 January 1960, the CDRJC narrow gauge lines inter-changed with the GNR. On 2 August 1956 S class 4-4-0 No 174 *Carrantuohill* arrives from the Omagh direction with a through train. On the right is the CDRJC coal stock and a narrow gauge bogie coach can just be seen. The leading coach is a D[1] side corridor Brake/1st, followed by a K[11] centre corridor Third.

ES Russell/Colour-Rail

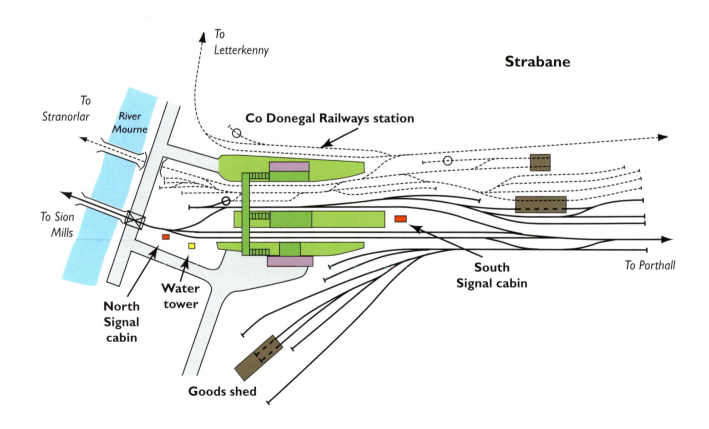

On 2 August 1958 Qs 4-4-0 No 135 arrives at Strabane with what is possibly the 3.25pm from Belfast and has a tender from one of the 1937 UGs. This particular locomotive had been given a major overhaul in October 1957 and is obviously still in superb condition. Although not graced with the sky blue livery of the S class (a decision regretted by Locomotive Engineer, Harry Wilson), this was an extremely handsome engine and, with No 131 preserved, we may yet see its like again. A station nameboard, similar to that on the up platform, is in the Ulster Folk and Transport Museum, Cultra, Co Down. The carriage is a G[3] centre corridor Brake/1st/2nd.   *ES Russell/Colour-Rail*

Two years earlier, on 2 August 1956, No 173 *Galteemore* has an up express at Strabane's Platform 1. This viewpoint shows the island platform (Platforms 2 and 3) and the CDRJC island platform beyond, with a typical string of County Donegal red wagons and a glimpse of a railcar. The footbridge linked all three platforms and on the right a gaggle of Donegal passengers descend from the footbridge to join the Belfast train.

ES Russell/Colour-Rail

At the Omagh end of Strabane, on Tuesday 22 May 1956, we have the unusual sight of double-headed PPs, Nos 12 and 50. The two coach train, even with the three vans (possibly the 12.25pm to Omagh), would hardly justify double-heading so we must assume that one engine is on its way to Enniskillen or Omagh, unless No 50 has failed. Note the PGs 0-6-0 shunting in the goods yard. The long Strabane footbridge had a corrugated roof in typical GNR fashion. *ES Russell/Colour-Rail*

Showing no headlamps of any kind, the double-header seen above pulls away from Strabane. The exit from the station was on Platform 1 and it was very tempting for passengers, arriving at Platform 2 with heavy luggage, to bypass the footbridge and use the barrow walk in the foreground. Staff were often placed at the foot of the steps to discourage this dangerous practice as the down train obscured a good view of approaching up trains. The clerestory brake on the left carries mail for Donegal, which will be transferred to CDRJC vans. Note the bread container on the rear of the down train. *ES Russell/Colour-Rail*

PPs 4-4-0 No 43 arrives at Strabane with an up local in August 1958, probably the 1.30pm Saturdays only. The carriages on the train are a K⁵ and a J⁴, plus two four-wheel vans. The fireman leans out to surrender the staff to the Strabane North signalman, whose box is just behind the photographer. The tracks in the foreground went to either side of the island platform. The sidings on the left interchanged with the narrow gauge.

Colour-Rail IR629

STRABANE TO DERRY

On 20 May 1960, a five car BUT railcar set is seen crossing the Foyle Bridge, just north of Strabane, on the 4.10pm Derry to Belfast service. The second coach of this train, B⁹ Buffet Car No 124, is featured in more detail on page 24.

JG Dewing

The three stations between Strabane and Derry were all in the Republic of Ireland and, after the division of the GNR on 1 October 1958, GNR staff at these stations were in the unusual situation of wearing CIÉ uniforms but having their stations served only by UTA trains. They also got the CIÉ weekly circular!

Porthall, seen here on 3 June 1963, was three miles from Strabane and the platform was on the up side. The station building was a GNR replacement of the original and resembled those on the Antrim branch. Note the small Customs hut, at the end of the fence.
Des FitzGerald

St Johnston, seen on the same date, was the most important of the three stations and had up and down platforms and a passing loop. It was the destination for many of the Customs-sealed wagons travelling to County Donegal from south of Dundalk. Provided they were sealed before crossing the border and not opened in

Northern Ireland, these consignments could pass through Customs without interference as 'Free to Free' traffic (a name deriving from the earlier Irish Free State). Because of this traffic, St Johnston also had a Customs post.
Des FitzGerald

About two miles beyond St Johnston, and five miles from Derry, was Carrigans. Until 1932 Derry to St Johnston was double track but latterly only the down side platform was in use. The rather utilitarian concrete building here was of inter-war construction and intended to accomodate a Customs hall. The shadows indicate that the railcar has a Brewster's bread container in tow. *Des FitzGerald*

Following the west bank of the River Foyle, the Derry Road re-entered Northern Ireland just after Carrigans and arrived at the 'Maiden City'. Derry had an engine shed and an extensive goods yard but the passenger station was disappointingly cramped. Situated on Foyle Road, it consisted of a single island platform and was partly under the Craigavon Bridge, which crossed the Foyle. On 27 July 1963 S class 4-4-0 No 170 *Errigal* (although no nameplates were carried by this date) has the 12.55pm Saturdays-only to Belfast. The UTA had bought this engine from CIÉ the previous month. *Des FitzGerald*

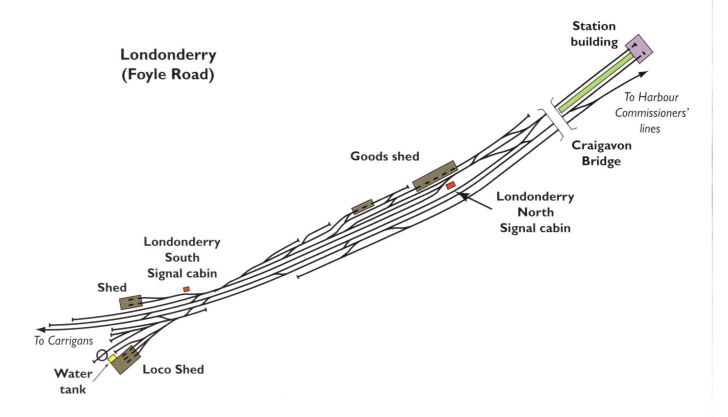

**Londonderry
(Foyle Road)**

Station
building

To Harbour
Commissioners'
lines

Craigavon
Bridge

Goods shed

Londonderry
North
Signal cabin

Londonderry
South
Signal cabin

Shed

To Carrigans

Water
tank

Loco Shed

This is the exterior of Foyle Road station on 2 September 1964. It was built by the INWR, in the Italianate style, to a design by Thomas Turner, replacing an earlier building. Convenient to the city centre, it attracted more Dublin than Belfast traffic as the NCC route to Belfast was shorter. The cars outside are a Morris Minor, an Austin A35, an Austin FX3 taxi and a Ford Consul.

Derek Young

DUBLIN

Having followed the GNR routes radiating from Belfast, we now move south to follow the services which commenced at Dublin and further north. Amiens Street station, Dublin, was the Headquarters of the Great Northern Railway and is still a very impressive station, much modernised in the last thirty years. Before the formation of the GNR in 1876, the lines to Howth, Drogheda and Oldcastle were owned by the Dublin and Drogheda Railway. In March 1875 the DDR had amalgamated with the Dublin and Belfast Junction Railway to form the Northern Railway, giving a main line running as far as Portadown. On 1 January 1876 the INWR joined the NR and then finally, in April 1876, the Ulster Railway joined the amalgam, which then adopted the much more dignified title 'Great Northern Railway (Ireland)'.

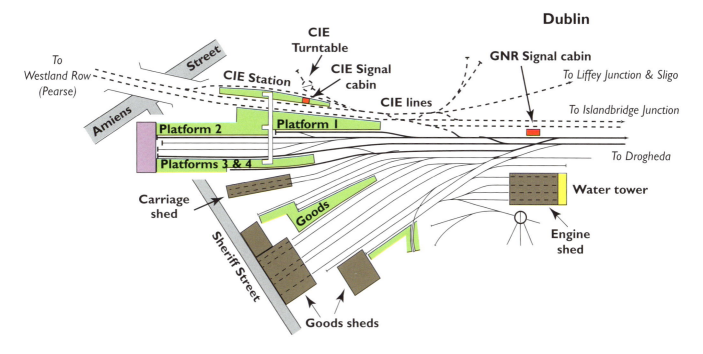

In July 1956 VS class 4-4-0 No 210 *Erne* approaches Amiens Street with an express from Belfast, probably the 11.50am, judging by the angle of the sun. On the right is Amiens Street shed and on the left the elevated signal cabin. Between the cabin and the GNR semaphore signals is a CIE electric signal. A small 0-6-0 shunts in the distance. The first coach on the train is a Corridor First, followed by B^4 Diner No 403 and a string of K^{15}s.

Keith Pirt

A lovely study of VS class 4-4-0 No 207 *Boyne*, preparing to depart from Platform 2 for Belfast with the 9.00am on Saturday 4 May 1957. The more observant readers will already have noticed a variation in the smoke deflectors of the VS class. On the first two fitted, Nos 206 and 209, the plates came up well above the side handrails (see page 83), which made it difficult to operate the valve visible here; this was for a steam lance used to clean tubes. The other three, as here, had plates just reaching the handrail. Visible beyond the canopy is the CIÉ part of the station.

Colour-Rail

On Sunday 14 June 1959, 4-4-0 Compound No 86 *Peregrine* moves along Platform 3 after being released from its train by a shunter (page 23, lower). It has possibly arrived on a GAA special from Belfast, as it is a UTA-owned engine and, if on a normal service train, would have been changed at Dundalk. Notice the nice clerestory Composite on the Howth local at Platform 2.

AG Cramp/Colour-Rail

At the adjacent platform 4, we see U class 4-4-0 No 197 *Lough Neagh* on the same occasion. For a period this engine was matched to this modern roller-bearing tender. It has what is probably a Howth local, with a four-compartment L[1] clerestory Brake/3rd leading. In the carriage sidings the GAA special is stabled, with K[15] No 138 easily identifiable. The roof of Sheriff Street goods shed is visible on the left.
AG Cramp/Colour-Rail IR150

A nice study of the now preserved No 85 *Merlin* sitting opposite Amiens Street shed in June 1961. At this time Merlin was the last surviving Compound and its normal duty was to be the 'ruck' or standby engine at Dundalk. It is buffered up to T2 4-4-2T No 3.

Note that by 1961 *Merlin* had an F type 4000 gallon tender from VS class 4-4-0 No 206 or 209, which had been scrapped in 1960. She ran with a similar tender in her early days of preservation.
Chris Gammell/Colour-Rail

Probably on the same day, No 3 is acting as station pilot and is shunting No 114, an L[13] Brake/3rd. This carriage was running as a BUT railcar trailer and is still in full GNR livery in 1961. It later

passed to the RPSI, who quickly removed the continental style corridor connections. Nos 3 and 143 were the last active CIÉ Glover tanks.
Keith Pirt

Photography at Amiens Street shed provided something of a challenge, particularly on sunny days like this June 1961 scene. Engines were normally stabled chimney towards Belfast, too close to the shed for a standard engine portrait, but the early morning sun was from the right leaving the bunkers in shadow. This line up has three 4-4-0s, S class No 174 *Carrantuohill*, Qs No 132 and VS No 208 *Lagan* (UTA No 58). On the right is CIÉ 0-6-2T No 673, built in 1933 and the last survivor of five.

Keith Pirt

The shed had four roads, passing through very narrow doors, a feature which caused the occasional serious injury. On 22 March 1959, SG2 0-6-0 No 184 simmers in the midday sun. These versatile engines were very popular with drivers. They steamed beautifully and could handle passenger trains and all but the heaviest goods trains. Their 5'1" driving wheels also made them suitable for excursion trains. The GNR contemplated building another batch of this 1915 design as late as 1954.   *Colour-Rail*

This general panorama from the end of Platform 1, on 14 June 1959, shows an impressive line up of gleaming blue engines at the shed. From left to right they are VS 4-4-0s Nos 208 and 207 and V 4-4-0 No 86. The shed closed in 2005, having been used for diesels since the end of steam in 1962. The carriages include two rakes of UTA stock, probably both on GAA specials. The distant rake has an L[11] Brake/3rd and a K[8] Third. The green carriage is L[10] No 369 (UTA No 470), the first GNR coach to get UTA livery, and is coupled to a K[11].   *AG Cramp/Colour-Rail*

A lovely study of Qs 4-4-0 No 131 coming off the turntable, which was at the right of the shed. It is May 1959 and the GNR spirit of pride in their engines is far from dead. This 1901 veteran emerged from a full overhaul at Dundalk Works in September 1958, thus ensuring that it survived until the end of steam and was preserved.
JG Dewing/Colour-Rail IR603

On the same turntable, S class 4-4-0 No 170 *Errigal* prepares to turn in August 1961. This engine emerged from its last major overhaul on 19 June 1959. That I can give as precise a date as this is down to the fact that Paddy Mallon of Dundalk Works kept a notebook where he recorded the dates into and out of the Works for all engines from late 1955. Engines repaired after the CIÉ takeover were not given lettering or crests, except for the very last, No 174. Paddy Mallon had kept a full set of transfers to mark this historic moment in 1960.
DH Ballantyne/Colour-Rail

Colour pictures of GNR goods trains around Dublin are rare, but in this undated scene UG 0-6-0 No 145 shunts bitumen tank wagons along MGWR tracks on the banks of the Royal Canal, adjacent to the Smith and Pearson Works. The UGs were little photographed by enthusiasts in GNR days but really showed their capabilities on the UTA section of the GNR after 1958.
Des FitzGerald

DUBLIN SUBURBAN

There were two suburban routes into Dublin from the north. Firstly, the Howth branch served a very popular middle class residential area on the Howth peninsula, with stations at Sutton and Howth. The east side of the peninsula was served by the Hill of Howth electric trams, also a GNR operation. The second route was along the main line to Malahide, Balbriggan and Drogheda. Today the Howth branch has been absorbed into the DART electrified network and trains now run through from Howth to Bray. Electrification has also advanced as far as Malahide and may eventually reach Drogheda.

In the steam age, the suburban services were dominated by the Glover 4-4-2Ts and, on 17 December 1960, No 143 is shunting a CIÉ carriage set into Platform 4. This was one of the last two CIÉ examples to remain active. It is worth noting that the tanks were always operated chimney towards Dublin, whilst tender engines were nearly always facing in the direction of travel. As always, someone will find an exception to this rule! *Des FitzGerald*

At Howth, on 6 July 1958, the fireman of T2 4-4-2T No 4 checks the trailing axle box, whilst waiting to return to Dublin. It is thought that operating with the chimney towards Dublin may have been to do with signals. Howth was a remarkably spartan station, with only one platform, a run round loop and a siding. Because this is a Sunday, the train has corridor stock, the leading vehicle being a G[6] side corridor Brake/1st/2nd.

Bruce Chapman collection/Colour-Rail

For years, off-peak services on the Howth branch were rostered for railcars F and G, which were built for this duty in 1938. These cars had two 102hp Gardner 6LW engines, driving different axles of the engine section. The entire train seated 164, more than a three-car AEC set, but in a lot less comfort. On 7 August 1955, railcar F is sitting in the Howth bay at Amiens Street (Platform 2). The carriage is No 322, a K[1] Third.

I Davidson/Colour-Rail IR572

On Sunday 2 June 1957, railcar F sits at Howth as its passengers queue to pass through the ticket barrier, some to enjoy the harbour (like those leaning over the railings on the left) and others to take a trip to the summit of the Hill of Howth on an electric tram. The Hill was very popular for Sunday outings from Dublin and the tram started just outside the station, as we shall shortly see.

FW Shuttleworth/Colour-Rail IR321

The Howth trains were also an ideal duty for the AEC railcars introduced in 1950, though they did not have a big presence on the branch until the BUT fleet arrived in 1957–58. They were also very popular on the Drogheda service, especially on short workings to Malahide and Balbriggan. From time to time a two car set ran without an intermediate trailer, as seen here in the carriage sidings at Amiens Street on 22 March 1959.

Colour-Rail

HILL OF HOWTH TRAMS

The Hill of Howth Tramway gave the GNR the unique distinction among railways in these islands in the 1950s, of simultaneously using steam, diesel, electric and horse traction on its lines. The tramway had opened in 1901, primarily as a tourist attraction, but it soon tapped an additional market of commuters wanting to travel from Sutton or Howth to other parts of the peninsula. There were ten tramcars.

We begin this short section on the trams with this view of No 4 at Howth on Sunday 15 March 1959. This was one of the first eight cars, which had Brill 22-E bogies and were built by Brush Electric in 1901. In the 1950s they were in the blue and cream bus/railcar livery. Howth station platform is just over the wall on the right and Howth signal cabin is just beyond the car. *John Langford*

Earlier the same day, the photographer had captured the scene at the summit (officially Hill of Howth) as No 4 stopped before continuing to Howth. Just visible on the left is the canopy of the passenger shelter with the conductor keeping watch. Attached to it was a parcels office and toilets. This building is now a private residence. Most of the buildings visible remain to this day. *John Langford*

A lovely picture of No 7 leaving Stella Maris on 29 March 1959. This was Easter Sunday that year and the passengers are enjoying an outing on a very fine afternoon. The motorcar on the right is a Mercedes, reflecting the relative prosperity of the Howth area. Stella Maris was just about the most southerly point on the tramway, which was mostly on its own reservation from Howth to here. Stella Maris passing loop is just out of sight round the corner and the tram has just joined Carrickbrack Road as it heads for Sutton.

David Soggee

Another view of No 4, this time on Easter Sunday 1959. The tram is heading down the Strand Road towards Sutton Cross. In the far distance is the stretch of road where the tram ran along the shore as it came down from Stella Maris. On windy days the spray from the sea often forced conductors to abandon their normal station on the open platform and retreat into the saloon.

David Soggee

At Sutton, the trams had a depot at the Dublin end of the station, on the up side. Leaving the depot to take up duty, trams crossed Station Road to access the station forecourt. Once loaded, they then passed through another gap in the station fence, as seen here, to re-cross Station Road and join their own reserved track to the right of the stone wall. On Saturday 13 September 1958 No 6 performs this manoeuvre. Sutton Cross is past the white house in the distance. The last trams ran on 31 May 1959. *David Soggee*

Cars 9 and 10 were heavier than Nos 1–8 and were designed for summer traffic. Seating 73, compared to 67 in the earlier cars, they were built in 1902 by GF Milnes on Peckham 14D-5 bogies. These heavy cars were tricky to handle and were banned from the steep Summit–Howth section until 1958, when they were fitted with diagonal cross-springs from withdrawn Nos 5 and 8. This reduced their tendency to derail on curves. No 10 was photographed at Sutton depot on 29 March 1959; the railway is in the background. These cars were never blue and cream. Both have been preserved, No 9 at the National Transport Museum, Howth, Dublin and No 10 at the National Tramway Museum, Crich, Derbyshire. *David Soggee*

DROGHEDA

We now leave the Howth branch and tramway to proceed up the main line to Drogheda. Drogheda has always been an important station. It was a terminus of the original Dublin and Drogheda Railway and, from 1850, was a junction for the Navan line, later extended to Kells and Oldcastle. It also had an important cement factory which generated much rail traffic. Today, Drogheda has become even more important as the chosen servicing centre for IÉ's new railcar fleet.

Viewed from a road bridge just south of Killester, near Dublin, VS 4-4-0 No 209 *Foyle* heads the 10.20am express for Belfast on Sunday 27 September 1958. This is a typical mainline train of the late 1950s, with a mixture of mahogany and blue/cream liveried carriages. A K[13] side corridor Third heads the rake.
JG Dewing/Colour-Rail IR317

Drogheda

To Dundalk

North signal cabin

Goods shed

To Navan & Oldcastle

River Boyne

Water tower →

Signal cabin

Goods shed

Engine shed

South signal cabin

Hill

Buckey's Sidings

To Dublin

Below: Looking slightly incongruous on a mainline railway, railbus No 1 sits at Drogheda's down platform in May 1957. Part of Drogheda's attractive station building can be seen in the background, with a porter checking parcels and there are lorries in the goods yard. No 1 was used on Oldcastle services, the branch being below the near side of the distant embankment. The junction faced Dublin so the railcar had to reverse out to the junction before heading for Navan.
FW Shuttleworth/Colour-Rail

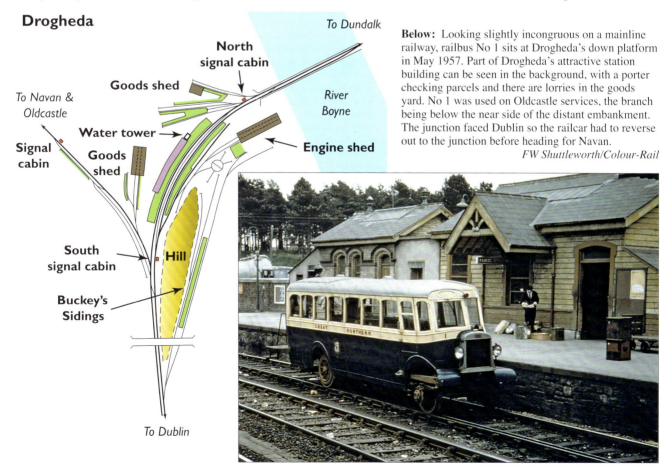

On 29 September 1958 V class 4-4-0 No 86 *Peregrine* heads south from Drogheda with a heavy train headed by the usual Corridor First and Diner No 403. Despite the 'UT' stenciled on the buffer, No 86 has one more day of GNR ownership to go before the company's assets are divided between CIÉ and the UTA. The goods store and South Cabin are prominent in the distance.

JG Dewing

Drogheda engine shed was located on the up side of the station, close to the Boyne Viaduct and still exists, serving as the wagon repair shed. It had two roads and was a scaled down version of the sheds at Dundalk and Dublin. Drogheda's allocation was usually a couple of 4-4-0s for the Oldcastle branch and lots of 0-6-0 goods engines. This July 1956 view shows a PPs 4-4-0 and three 0-6-0s, including PGs No 102 on the right. Note the North Cabin in the left background and the Departmental six-wheeler on the right.

Keith Pirt

There was a turntable just to the east of the shed and this is where the now-preserved S class 4-4-0 No 171 *Slieve Gullion* was photographed one evening in August 1958. The engine is carrying a single headlamp denoting a local passenger train and has probably worked an evening suburban train down from Dublin. The wagons in the background are in Buckey's sidings.

Colour-Rail IR174

VS class 4-4-0 No 209 *Foyle* pulls out of Drogheda with an evening express for Belfast on Wednesday 27 August 1958. This was possibly the 6.25pm from Dublin. Drogheda was on a 90° curve with a 15mph restriction. No 209 was one of the two VSs with the taller smoke deflectors. The leading coach looks like a K[17] side corridor Third.

Colour-Rail

OLDCASTLE BRANCH

One line that has hitherto featured little in books is the 39½ mile GNR(I) branch to Oldcastle. This was opened to Navan in 1850, to Kells in 1853 and to Oldcastle in 1863. It closed to passengers in April 1958 but in 2005 is still open for goods as far as Navan. Goods traffic beyond Navan ceased in March 1963.

We start our coverage of the branch with this view of Railcar A at Drogheda in April 1956, preparing to work the 3.40pm service to Oldcastle. Although the tailboard shows that we are looking at the rear of the train, it will first run past the photographer, towards Dublin, before joining the branch. Railcar A had been the mainstay of the Banbridge–Scarva branch until its closure in 1955. It then spent three years on the Oldcastle line before transferring the the Derry Road in 1958. This view shows the island platform at Drogheda with passengers waiting for a train to Dublin.

TJ Edgington/Colour-Rail IR130

Oldcastle

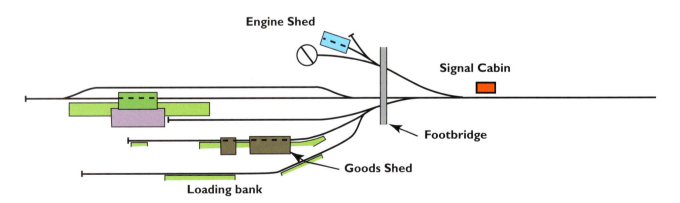

Some passenger services were steam-hauled and handled by engines of the P, PP and QL classes. In October 1954 PPs 4-4-0 No 71 has just arrived at Oldcastle from Drogheda, the angle of the sun suggesting the 3.40pm train, though this service was normally a railbus or railcar. Like Fintona, Belturbet and Warrenpoint, Oldcastle had a short train shed. A passenger and his son chat to the driver before the engine is turned, ready for the 5.10pm return.

Ray Oakley/Colour-Rail IR602

The next sequence of pictures were taken on an RBAI Railway Society railtour on 28 April 1962, slightly beyond the GNR era, but providing the last opportunity to cover this line in colour. This is Oldcastle station viewed from the opposite direction to the previous picture. The engine has already turned to face Drogheda. This railtour was organised by staff and pupils of a school, the Royal Belfast Academical Institution. *Richard Whitford*

A few moments earlier, the engine had turned. This view shows the locomotive moving back off the turntable, just visible on the left. The locomotive used on this trip was SG 0-6-0 No 177, which was well-cleaned for the occasion. This engine was scrapped the following November.

Richard Whitford

Right: The first station out of Oldcastle was Virginia Road, though in this view the road bridge obscures the station itself. The width of the bridge suggests that there was once a run round loop or siding. The young man on the left is Joe Cassells, the co-author of the Colourpoint book, *Forty Shades of Steam.*

Richard Whitford

Below: The next station was Kells, seen here looking towards Oldcastle. The level crossing was at the down end of the station. Originally an 'H' section building, the gap between the two wings has later been filled by a waiting room. For ten years, this station was a terminus, the railway having reached there in 1853.

Richard Whitford

Above: A second view of Kells, this time taken from the signal cabin. Note the extensive goods yard on the right. The two carriages on the train were GNR centre-corridor vehicles. They were No 283, a K^{10} Third, originally a Tea Car and (nearer the camera) No 346, virtually identical but an L^{10} Brake/3rd.
Denis Grimshaw

Left: The tour next stopped at Ballybeg, which was little more than a single platform at a level crossing, though there was also a goods siding at the down end. Today, a railtour on a line which was closed to passenger traffic would be unlikely. How different things were in 1962! Note the down home and up starter signals on one post.
Richard Whitford

Between Ballybeg and Navan there were four level crossings designated as railcar stopping points, though these were closed in 1956. Approaching Navan, the MGWR route from Kingscourt joined the GNR route at Navan West Junction. The two lines then ran in parallel to Navan Junction. Between these two points was Commons Road Crossing, seen here on the outward trip, so we are facing Oldcastle and the Midland line is on the right. Note the pair of home signals in the distance, one for each route.
Richard Whitford

Navan Junction was where the Midland line diverged off to Dunboyne, Clonsilla Junction and Dublin. This view, facing Drogheda, shows the Midland station and the Dublin line. GNR trains stopped here between 1941 and 1946. Today there is a strong possibility that the Dublin to Navan line may be reopened as a suburban service. Note the very light MGWR flat-bottom rail, compared to the GNR bullhead, and the very low signal, for sighting below the demolished footbridge. The cabin is a GNR one.

Richard Whitford

The GNR station at Navan was at the Drogheda side of Navan Junction. The RBAI tour stopped here to take water on the return journey from Oldcastle. Although the train obscures the station in this view, we can see the signal cabin, loading bank and goods store.

Richard Whitford

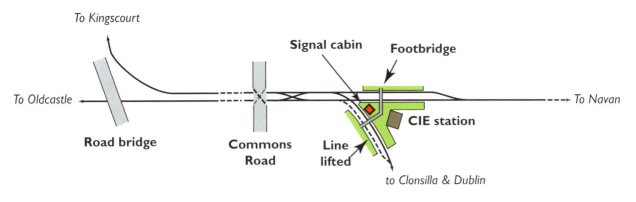

Navan Junction

To Kingscourt

To Oldcastle

Road bridge

Commons Road

Signal cabin

Footbridge

CIE station

Line lifted

To Navan

to Clonsilla & Dublin

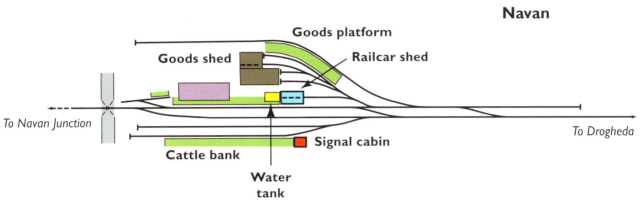

Navan

Goods platform

Goods shed

Railcar shed

To Navan Junction

Cattle bank

Water tank

Signal cabin

To Drogheda

The same general scene, viewed from the opposite end of the cattle bank. It is not totally clear why the engine has moved to this end of the train, as the water tower was at the other end. Modellers can have a field day with the signal on the left!

Richard Whitford

Navan signal cabin, viewed from the Drogheda end of the platform, with No 177 taking water on the return journey. Note the twin CIE stencils on the tender tank, rather than the bufferbeam. No 177 was a Drogheda engine.   *Richard Whitford*

Drogheda in July 1956, showing an Oldcastle branch train coming off the branch. The engine is again No 177, showing that this was a Drogheda engine even six years before the railtour. This is probably the 7.45am from Oldcastle, at that time the only steam passenger working. The leading carriage is No 2, a unique Lavatory Brake/ Composite, built in 1911 as a slip coach, but no longer one by 1956.
Keith Pirt

DUNLEER AND ARDEE

We now return to the main line as we head towards Dundalk. This section included the short branch to Ardee, which closed to passengers as long ago as 1934 but remained open for goods until 1975.

About ten miles north of Drogheda was Dunleer, seen here in a view facing north in September 1958. A goods train is departing for Drogheda hauled by NQGs 0-6-0 No 38, wearing 'slow stopping goods' headlamps. This was a train from Ardee which had been shunted to the down line to be overtaken and is about to cross to the up line. The five-strong NQG class were built in 1911 as a Nasmyth Wilson version of the QG class. No 38 was one of two originally fitted with the unsuccessful Phoenix superheater, quickly removed. *JG Dewing/Colour-Rail*

Another member of the NQGs class, No 112, has the 11.30am goods from Ardee at Dromin Junction on 23 May 1958. This was the junction for the Ardee branch and the main line towards Dundalk is on the right. Nos 38 and 112 both passed to CIÉ in 1958. The other three members of the class, Nos 3, 39 and 109, were rebuilt as LQGs and passed to the UTA. *TJ Edington/Colour-Rail IR631*

A good general view of Ardee goods yard on 20 July 1960 with 0-6-0 No 148, one of the five UGs built in 1948, shunting the daily goods. At this time Ardee still offered some cattle traffic. The factory in the background brought much business to the railway and was one of the factors in the branch remaining open for goods until 3 November 1975. Passenger services had been withdrawn on 3 June 1934. The track in the centre of the picture leads to the former passenger station. *B Hilton/Colour-Rail*

DUNDALK

In GNR days, and for many years afterwards, Dundalk was a very interesting place for railway enthusiasts. Because it was the engineering headquarters of the company, it was always worth looking out for newly shopped engines or engines waiting repair. The station itself was busy with interchange between the main line and the Irish North and earlier with the Dundalk Newry and Greenore Railway.

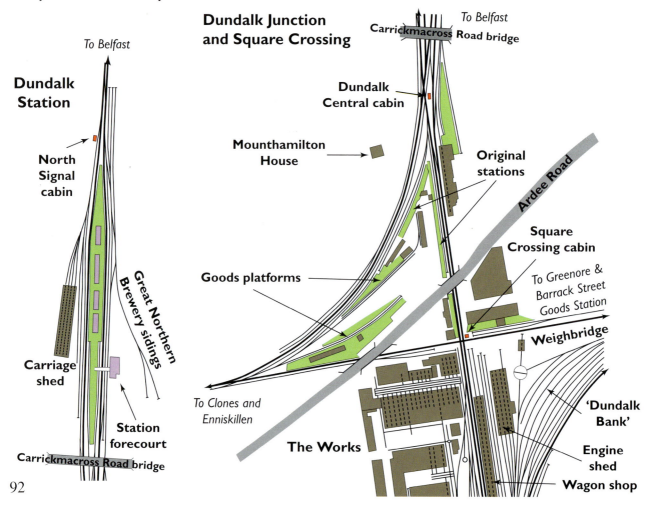

Our first picture at Dundalk shows Qs 4-4-0 No 131 heading south with the heavy 12.45pm to Dublin in November 1961. The steam engine was substituting for the normal diesel locomotive. The train has just passed under the Ardee Road bridge and is passing the general stores on the right with its first floor offices. In the far distance is Dundalk Central cabin. The train will shortly be passing the Works, which are behind the photographer on the down side of the line. *R Biddick/Colour-Rail IR566*

Dundalk engine shed was virtually identical to the one at Amiens Street, save that Dundalk shed was rendered and had a clock. In this July 1956 view, it is 9.10 in the morning and U class 4-4-0 No 198 *Lough Swilly* is being prepared to work the down 'Bundoran Express' forward from Dundalk. It is booked to arrive in Dundalk at 9.58am and leave again at 10.05am. To the left of this picture is the wagon repair shop. The shed was on the up side of the main line *Keith Pirt*

About 25 minutes after the previous picture, No 198 is still raising steam and V class 4-4-0 compound No 85 *Merlin* has appeared. As the engine does not appear to be in steam, it is possible that the photographer has persuaded someone to pull *Merlin* out of the shed for a photograph. Today the engine shed is a Bus Éireann garage.

Keith Pirt

Coal for GNR locomotives was stored in staiths which were immediately behind the photographer in the previous photograph. Beyond the coal staiths was a set of sidings known as the 'Dundalk bank' Here dead engines and spare tenders were stored, some to be resurrected and taken into the Works; others like JT 2-4-2T No 90 in July 1956 had run their last mile and faced only the cutter's torch.   *Keith Pirt*

Although you could be forgiven for thinking this is the Works area, the photographer is standing inside the back of the engine shed and looking towards the general stores on the opposite side of the branch to Barrack Street goods yard. Stored beside the stores is railcar C¹. In this June 1961 shot, SG3 0-6-0 No 117 is under the shear legs. It was scrapped in 1963.

David Soggee

Opposite: Assuming that this is the same July morning, we can conjecture that it is now about 9.45am and that S class 4-4-0 No 170 *Errigal* has just worked down from Dublin on the 7.35am to Dundalk. It has now run back from the passenger station and is moving up to the turntable which was located on the east side of the shed. No 170 is looking a little unkempt after a hard run. It will probably work back on the 12.50pm. Note the Dundalk-made injector, with its inelegant bracket, below the cab footstep. The tender has been transferred from one of the 1937-built UG 0-6-0s.

Keith Pirt

Dundalk passenger station was, and still is, an impressive location. The station comprises a large wide island platform with up and down faces and an up bay. On 16 June 1962, U class 4-4-0 No 204 *Antrim* is in the bay platform known as the Enniskillen bay, with a morning local train to Dublin. Note the coaches stored in the carriage sidings beyond the down platform. The large footbridge provided the only access to the platforms, a layout favoured in many English stations.

Irwin Pryce/Colour-Rail

This is the down platform face on 18 August 1963 showing more detail of the carriage sidings. Beyond the platform is Dundalk North Cabin and in the far distance the South Armagh mountains beckon, with Slieve Gullion itself prominent. Dundalk had, and still has, the typical GNR yellow, purple and black decorative brickwork.

John Langford

Railway modellers are probably well aware of Tony Miles' superb O gauge model of 'Adavoyle', representing an imaginary GNR station based on features of both Dundalk and Strabane. The real Adavoyle was a closed station about eight miles north of Dundalk and is seen here on 31 May 1963. The photographer was on the footplate of a northbound goods, hauled by an SG3 class 0-6-0, which had been slowed to a crawl by the adverse signal ahead. It did 'come off' before he had to stop! The signal cabin is the stone building on the left, with the pitched roof.

JG Dewing

THE ENTERPRISE

The GNR had two named trains, both of which appeared after 1945. One was the 'Bundoran Express' which we have referred to earlier and will meet again later. The other is the better known 'Enterprise' which was launched in August 1947 as a non-stop express service between Belfast and Dublin. Up to 1965 the 'Enterprise' name was applied only to two daily non-stop trains in each direction but since then it has become a generic brand name for all through trains. These pictures feature the train in GNR days.

The earliest view we have shows the train in 1948 when the V class compounds were the main motive power. This shows No 84 *Falcon* just north of Knock Bridge with the Belfast-based set on the 5.30pm down train. In the morning it had operated the 10.30am up service. By mid-1948 *Falcon* was the only Compound to have received a Belpaire firebox. *AD Hutchinson/Colour-Rail IR563*

Sometimes the lighter Dublin-based set was hauled by one of the older S class engines. On 15 July 1949, No 170 hauls the 5.15pm up service towards Knock Bridge, south of Portadown. This six coach set comprises an L¹⁴ Brake/3rd, two K¹⁵s, a Diner, a C² First and a D⁵ Brake/1st. All first class accomodation was in side corridor and all third class was in open coaches. The S class did not normally wear the horseshoe headboard seen on No 84 above. *AD Hutchinson/Colour-Rail*

From late 1950 to 1953 the 'Enterprise' worked right through to Cork, a CIÉ set working in the opposite direction. This interesting view, on 16 July 1951, shows the CIE set approaching Knock Bridge, near Portadown. It would have left Cork earlier in the day and is now the 2.30pm from Dublin. The engine is VS class 4-4-0 No 208 *Lagan* and the set has been strengthened by two GNR coaches.

AD Hutchinson/Colour-Rail

Although the Dublin-based 'Enterprise' was dieselised in the early 1950s using a four car AEC set, heavy traffic occasionally led to steam substitution, as seen here. (The wording on the headboard indicates a Dublin-based working.) The Belfast set remained steam until 1957 and its headboard was worded as in the picture above. VS 4-4-0 No 209 *Foyle* hauls the 4.45pm up service over the square crossing at Dundalk in May 1957. Note that the third class accomodation is at the Dublin end on this train, as an L^{14} heads the formation.

TB Owen/Colour-Rail IR180

From 1957 the 'Enterprise' was rostered for BUT railcar sets. Reflecting the patronage, the Dublin-based set was usually only four car, as seen in this view of the 4.45pm up working at Adelaide on 16 May 1960. By this date, the CIE 'Enterprise' was a rather untidy combination of three liveries, the B^9 Buffet Car being a hasty conversion to BUT operation, without repainting. The rear vehicle is No 906.

JG Dewing

DUNDALK TO CLONES

The first part of the Irish North was the line from Dundalk to Clones, continuing on to Enniskillen and Omagh. Irish North trains commenced at the up side bay platform in Dundalk and then diverged at Dundalk Junction to pass the old Irish North Western station and head for Clones. Branches diverged from the line to Carrickmacross and Cootehill, and in earlier days to Armagh. Unfortunately, few colour slides seem to have been taken at intermediate stations between Dundalk and Clones so I am using pictures from an Irish Railway Record Society (IRRS) enthusiast tour over the route on 31 December 1959 using an ex-GNR two car AEC diesel train.

This tour was the last passenger train to run over the Irish North, which had remained open for goods after the ending of regular passenger services in October 1957. The tour ran down the Carrickmacross branch before heading for Castleblayney.

Essexford was the intermediate station on the branch and it still exists much as seen here. This view from a nearby overbridge is looking back towards Dundalk.   *John Langford*

The Carrickmacross branch diverged from the Irish North at Inniskeen and was 6½ miles long. This view shows the train after arrival at Carrickmacross. The covered train shed is reminiscent

of those at Bundoran, Oldcastle and Warrenpoint. The two railcars used on the tour were Nos 608 and 609. CIE added the letters 'G' and 'N' on either side of GNR carriage numbers.   *John Langford*

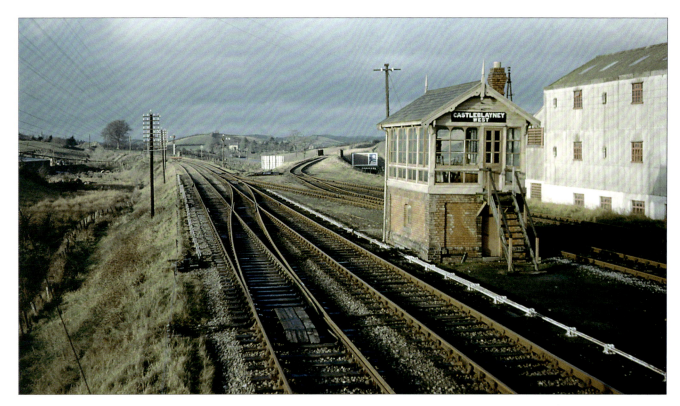

Fading light meant that this picture at Ballybay was the last colour shot that was possible on the trip. Ballybay was seven miles past Castleblayney and nearly 25 from Dundalk. This, too, was a sizeable town, with a conveniently sited railway station. Here our photographer scrambled up the hill hoping to get a good vantage point for a picture of the station, which is to the left. Unfortunately trees made this impossible so he opted for this view looking in the Clones direction. Note the distant flooding.

John Langford

Clones was a very important junction on the Irish North, with the line from Belfast and Armagh arriving from the northeast and a branch to Cavan diverging at the southwest end. In July 1956 SG3 0-6-0 No 40 is station pilot and is adding the through pilgrim coach from Belfast, Armagh and Monaghan to the rear of the down 'Bundoran Express'. The carriage is a J^4 Brake Composite, designed for use as a through coach. On the right is Clones shed, a roundhouse similar to that at Portadown.

Keith Pirt

Opposite: A very good view of the west end of Castleblayney, looking towards Clones. The stub of the former line to Armagh is visible in the right distance. This line closed as early as 1926, the last part of it becoming the Keady branch from Armagh seen earlier (pages 52/3). Castleblayney was the largest town on the route and one is tempted to wonder how a rail service would be supported today, given the growth of long-distance commuting to Dublin. The repainted point rodding was a sure sign of pending closure! *John Langford*

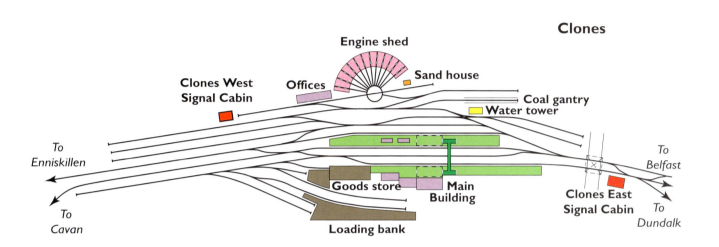

One of the services to Clones was rostered for a diesel train. In the winter timetable this was the 11.15am from Belfast, which reached Clones at 1.30pm and worked back at 2.50pm. This train was photographed at Clones in April 1956. The trailer is either No 8 or No 9, one of the 'mules' which had a small driving cab, and at the far end will be No 617. On the same platform, directly behind the railcar set, is a steam train for Cavan. The engines in the shed include JT class 2-4-2T No 91, which normally worked the Belturbet branch. *TJ Edgington/Colour-Rail*

101

A relaxed scene at the west end of Clones in April 1956. This is probably the 12.25pm railbus service to Cavan, a good lead in to the next group of pictures. With four passengers visible, the viability of this train must be in some doubt. Meanwhile, the crew have a quiet smoke while awaiting departure. Over the fence, full cattle wagons and empty bread containers wait to leave for Belfast on the 12.40pm 'Shipper'.

Colour-Rail

This photograph is interesting in two respects. Firstly it shows the shed area from an unusual angle looking towards the town. Secondly, it was taken in August 1958, nearly a year after passenger services had ended, but the GNR was still operating goods trains. The engine is LQGs No 158 and it has been in Clones since 7.00am, having worked the daily 4.00am from Dundalk. Its day included a trip to Cavan at 9.30am, returning at 3.00pm and then leaving for Dundalk at 7.20pm.

M Burnett/Colour-Rail

Looking towards the Sacred Heart Church, as in the previous picture, PPs 4-4-0 No 75 moves cautiously onto the turntable on a July day in 1956. This class of engine shared honours with the U class on most Irish North passenger services. Notice the wagons of discarded ash in the background. As with all roundhouse layouts, the only access to the shed was by the turntable. Woe betide any unfortunate driver who deposited his engine in the pit and brought all operations to a halt!

Keith Pirt

BELTURBET AND CAVAN

The Clones to Cavan branch was just over 15 miles long and, after the closure to passengers of the CIÉ route from Cavan to Dublin in 1947, provided Cavan's only rail passenger service. It was worked by a mixture of railbuses, railcars and steam trains. Six and a half miles from Cavan, the Belturbet branch diverged at Ballyhaise. The chief significance of this 4¼ mile branch was that it made an end-on connection with the Cavan and Leitrim section of CIÉ at Belturbet, with onwards transfer of goods and passengers. Passenger services ended in October 1957 but the goods continued until the closure of the narrow gauge in March 1959.

Ballyhaise Junction in August 1956, looking towards Clones. Railcar C¹ is actually the mainline train despite appearances! It made two round trips daily at 10.00am and 12.25pm out of Clones and this is likely the second of these. The branch set was always steam and comprised one bogie coach and a van. Normally worked by 2-4-2T No 91, shedded at Clones, the relief engine was normally a PPs, like No 107 here.

Chris Banks collection/Colour-Rail

A month earlier we see the more normal arrangement, with No 91 waiting departure for Belturbet. This was the last JT class 2-4-2T to remain in service and it continued to be used by CIÉ as a shunter in Dublin into the early 1960s. The up platform building, and the station master's house seen here, were still there when I last visited Ballyhaise in 2003.

Keith Pirt

On the same day, we see No 91, with a single headlamp indicating 'branch goods' sitting near the goods tranship shed at Belturbet, out of view to the left of the photographer. Visible are the passenger train shed and, in the right background, the goods store, now a community hall. Note the Cavan and Leitrim wagon, as some of the tracks are narrow gauge. *Keith Pirt*

A pleasant view at Cavan in 1956. The photographer is facing Clones and P5'6" 4-4-0 No 105 has just arrived with a passenger train, which has a string of cattle wagons attached (since these were 'fitted', the 'ordinary passenger train' lamp code is correct). The GNR had a goods station and engine shed on the Clones side of the CIÉ station. The goods store is just visible above the cattle wagons.

There were steam hauled trains from Clones at 10.25am, 3.00pm and 6.15pm, but this is probably the 10.25. The carriages are a J[6] and an ex-LNWR Corridor Third. Note the CIÉ wagons. *Colour-Rail*

Opposite: An archetypal branch line scene at Belturbet in July 1956. No 91 awaits its next duty with its carriage partly in the train shed. With Belturbet station now beautifully restored, even to the extent of a track being laid, and with JT 2-4-2T No 93 preserved in the Ulster Folk and Transport Museum, it would be technically possible to recreate this scene today, but perhaps it is best left to the modellers.   *Keith Pirt*

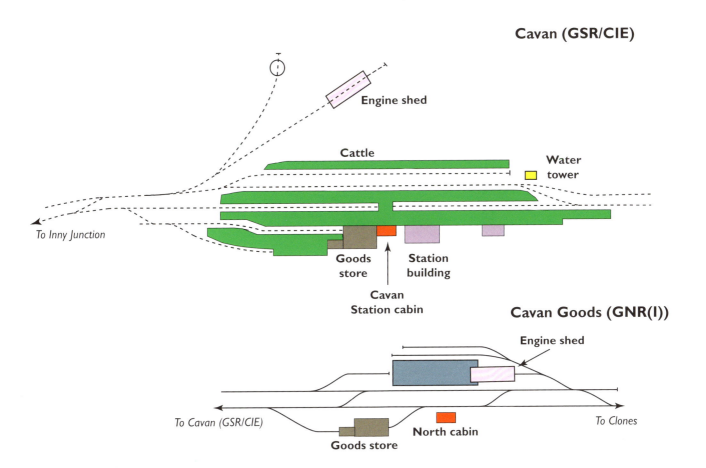

Cavan (GSR/CIE)

Engine shed

Cattle

Water tower

Goods store

Station building

Cavan Station cabin

Cavan Goods (GNR(I))

Engine shed

To Cavan (GSR/CIE)

To Clones

North cabin

Goods store

In August 1956 we see railcar C[1] with the 1.20pm to Clones in the bay. These railcars often hauled a small trailer with a pitched roof and one can be seen here with the roof raised for loading. Cavan was a CIÉ station and had an unusual layout with two platforms separated by one track and joined in the centre by a walkway which created two bays (see diagram). Beyond the railcar can be seen the carriages of the earlier steam train and that track was the only one which joined the two systems. In the right background is the CIÉ engine shed.

Chris Banks collection/Colour-Rail IR281

ENNISKILLEN

Returning to Clones we now head down the Irish North main line to Enniskillen. Unfortunately, no colour has yet appeared showing any of the intermediate stations. At Enniskillen, the GNR met the northern end of the Sligo, Leitrim and Northern Counties Railway. The station was built on a tight curve which turned more than 120 degrees in a few hundred yards.

U class 4-4-0 No 199 *Lough Derg* is at the east end of Enniskillen on 7 May 1957, about to depart with a Clones train. The leading vehicle is an I⁷ or I⁸ Tricomposite. The track to the right of the

engine's buffer allowed engines to bypass the passenger station. Small blue engines like this are a deep, personal memory for me of the GNR at Enniskillen. *Colour-Rail*

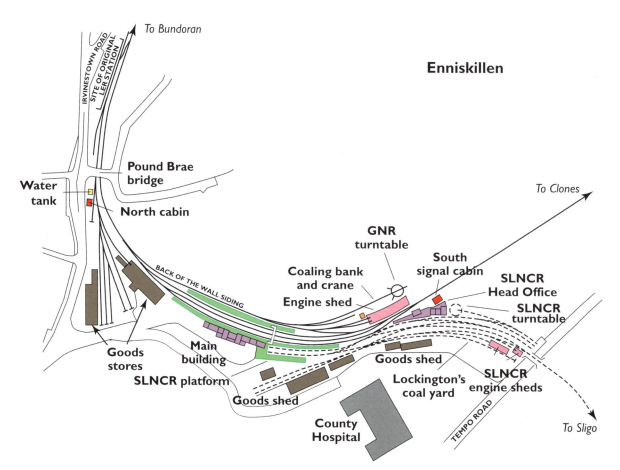

Looking in the opposite direction from this same point gave a view of Enniskillen shed. Here, on the same date, are U class 4-4-0 No 204 *Antrim*, which has probably just come off the train seen opposite, and LQGs 0-6-0 No 161, which is being prepared for the evening goods to Derry. The red building to the right of the Clones line is the headquarters of the SLNCR and the Sligo line was just out of shot to the right.   *Colour-Rail*

In September 1957, U class 4-4-0 No 196 *Lough Gill* basks in the morning sunshine as it prepares to work a down train, probably the 7.15am to Omagh. The LNWR-style six-wheeler was originally from the DNGR and was the Enniskillen breakdown van. It ended its days at Portadown shed, equipped with jacks, packing blocks, etc.   *Colour-Rail*

On an earlier occasion, this time in 1956, we see a heavy goods engine at Enniskillen. No 119 is an LQGs 0-6-0 and has very probably worked in on the overnight goods from Derry. It will return to the maiden city at 9.30 that evening. Other engines in view are an SG class 0-6-0 (left) for the Belfast goods, a PPs 4-4-0 (background) and U class 4-4-0 No 204 *Antrim* (right). Note, too, the ancient drover's brake van.   *Colour-Rail IR95*

On a wet day in September 1957, we have the view from the 12.00 noon for Omagh at Enniskillen showing No 603 on the Belfast diesel. In the summer months the AEC diesel set seen earlier at Clones worked through to Enniskillen. It left Belfast at 9.00am, reached Enniskillen at 11.37am and left again at 12.30pm.

This set has a standard K[15] trailer and probably No 602 at the Clones end. Note the fitted cattle and bread wagons on the rear of the steam train. The middle road was vital for running round trains.
Ray Oakley/Colour-Rail

This sad view of Enniskillen was taken about 1960 with the remaining track very overgrown with weeds, but nevertheless gives a very good overall view of the station. Only the centre road remains. We are looking towards Omagh and on the left is the Sligo bay. In the far distance is the goods shed, the last part of the station to survive. To the right of the up platform is the trackbed of the 'Back of the Wall' siding. In 1960 the track was being lifted from Clones towards Bundoran Junction. *Elder, courtesy S Johnston*

This is LQGs 0-6-0 No 111 on the lifting train at Enniskillen about 1960. This is at the north end of the station and the engine is in the small siding beside the North Cabin, probably taking water. The old carriage in the siding may have been serving as sleeping accomodation for the lifting gang. The bridge behind carried a steeply climbing minor road known as the Pound Brae which often taxed my uncle's Ford Zephyr. The bridge was demolished later and the Pound Brae was then accessed from a new road near the goods store. *Elder, courtesy S Johnston*

Taken on the same occasion, this view is from the Pound Brae bridge looking down at the Omagh line, which is the near track. The waste ground was the site of the original Londonderry and Enniskillen Railway station. The engine is in a siding and the remains of the old platform are behind it. In the background is Forthill Street which forked to Mill Street and the Irvinestown Road. *Elder, courtesy S Johnston*

BUNDORAN BRANCH

Between Enniskillen and Omagh the Bundoran branch diverged at Bundoran Junction, near the village of Kilskeery, for a 35 mile jaunt to the seaside. One of the more important stations en route was Pettigo which was the destination of the pilgrim trains. After 1945 the pilgrim train was honoured with the name 'Bundoran Express', not so much because of its speed (though it did touch 60 mph in places) but because much of its journey was non-stop. The down train left Dublin at 8.45am and after a stop at Dundalk around 10.00am to change engines and reverse direction, it reached Clones at 11.17am. There was then a 33 minute wait at Clones for the Buffet Car to be removed and the through coach from Armagh to be added. To avoid Customs stops, the 'Express' then ran through Northern Ireland non-stop to Pettigo, passing Enniskillen at 12.27pm.

Pettigo was reached at 1.04pm and there the pilgrims would detrain on one platform, whilst the returning pilgrims boarded the up 'Bundoran Express' on the other. The fleet of buses which had brought the returning pilgrims from Lough Derg then conveyed the new lot to their island destination. Meanwhile the remaining passengers were mostly conventional holidaymakers and reached Bundoran at 2.00pm. The up 'Express' had left Bundoran at 12.25 but, as the pilgrimage placed a lot of emphasis on fasting, the attaching of the Buffet Car at Clones was really of little or no use, as the pilgrims' fasting actually continued until midnight. Dublin was reached at 5.45pm, over six hours from Bundoran.

These rostering arrangements required two complete trains and two locomotives daily, all for the sake of the up train leaving Bundoran an hour and a half before the down one arrived. In later years, when the train terminated at Omagh, one train sufficed but this upset arrangements on the island.

Ballyshannon was the last station before Bundoran and, on Thursday 6 June 1957, PGs 0-6-0 No 10 has the seemingly rather untaxing duty of the down goods. This had left Enniskillen at 5.50am and reached Ballyshannon at 9.45am. To set the record straight on the load, it will already have dropped wagons at Irvinestown, Kesh, Pettigo and Belleek and may have just deposited the Ballyshannon wagons in the goods shed on the left. It will need to be away at 10.10am to clear the section for the 9.10am railcar from Enniskillen, due at 10.22am, and to reach Bundoran without delaying the 10.30am up passenger. *Colour-Rail*

Bundoran

This view from the road bridge, on 7 July 1959, gives a panoramic view of the station layout at Ballyshannon, with the tracks somewhat overgrown after nearly two years of neglect. We are looking towards Bundoran, with the main building and goods yard on the town or up side. The signal cabin was on the down side. The green, corrugated iron hut was the Customs building.
David Soggee

PPs 4-4-0 No 50 has just arrived at Bundoran in September 1957 with what is probably the 2.35pm from Bundoran Junction. As the 2.05pm from Enniskillen, this had run as a double-headed combined train for Omagh and Bundoran as far as the Junction before splitting and making a connection with the 1.45pm from Omagh. Bundoran had a long platform, with two faces, with the signal cabin at the far end. On the right is the goods loading bank and the large stone building is the engine shed.
JM Chamney/Colour-Rail

At an unknown date, but probably in the summer of 1957, U class 4-4-0 No 201 *Meath* has arrived with the down 'Bundoran Express' and has shunted back to clear the crossover. No 201 will shunt the coaches to the far side of the platform for the following day's up 'Express' and then turn before retiring to the shed for the night. This slide was one of the two GNR slides referred to in the introduction.
ColourViews 1054

POST 1958

We end the book with a few views reflecting the changing scene on the southern half of the system after the GNR was divided between the UTA and CIÉ on 1 October 1958.

The modern railcar fleet was initially divided equally between the two new owners but, in a bit of horse trading, the UTA acquired BUT railcars Nos 702 and 902 in exchange for its share of the cement wagons which it did not need. On 21 June 1959 we see evidence that CIÉ was using its BUT railcars on Howth suburban services. The GNR envisaged their use on long distance trains. With two '900 series' cars, an F^{16} Composite and an L^{13} Brake Third, there is certainly plenty of first class accomodation – 48 seats out of a total of 182!

AG Cramp/Colour-Rail

The changeover period resulted in all sorts of odd livery combinations. At Gormanston viaduct on 15 May 1959 we see a down two-car AEC set, with the rear car in CIÉ livery but hauling a J^{11} Tricomposite Brake in mahogany livery. The leading car looks to be No 609.

JG Dewing

By 18 March 1962 virtually all the ex-GNR stock had been painted into CIÉ livery and on hauled trains CIÉ-designed carriages were running alongside the GNR types. On this train the first and fourth carriages are GNR K^{15}s but the fifth vehicle is a CIÉ one. GNR steam engines were not reliveried and No 174 *Carrantuohill* is in rather unkempt blue. This engine was the last to be overhauled at Dundalk and, when outshopped in June 1960 (as explained on page 75) was given GNRB crests – an appropriate gesture to mark the end of an era.

Chris Gammell/Colour-Rail